BRAZIL

WHAT EVERYONE NEEDS TO KNOW®

BRAZIL

WHAT EVERYONE NEEDS TO KNOW®

RIORDAN ROETT

OXFORD
UNIVERSITY PRESS

Oxford University Press is a department of the University of Oxford. It furthers the University's objective of excellence in research, scholarship, and education by publishing worldwide. Oxford is a registered trade mark of Oxford University Press in the UK and certain other countries.

Published in the United States of America by Oxford University Press
198 Madison Avenue, New York, NY 10016, United States of America.

CIP data is on file at the Library of Congress
ISBN 978–0–19–022452–3 (hbk.); 978–0–19–022453–0 (pbk.)

1 3 5 7 9 8 6 4 2
Printed by R.R. Donnelley, United States of America

In memory of Werner Baer, Dedicated Economics Professor, passionate Brazilianist, good friend and colleague for many decades. May he rest in peace.

CONTENTS

ACKNOWLEDGMENTS

I am grateful for the professional research and assistance of Lorena Americano Valente, Gonzalo E. Aguilera, and John R. McGeoch from SAIS and the editing and production support at Oxford University press of David McBride and Prabhu Chinnasamy.

BRAZIL

WHAT EVERYONE NEEDS TO KNOW®

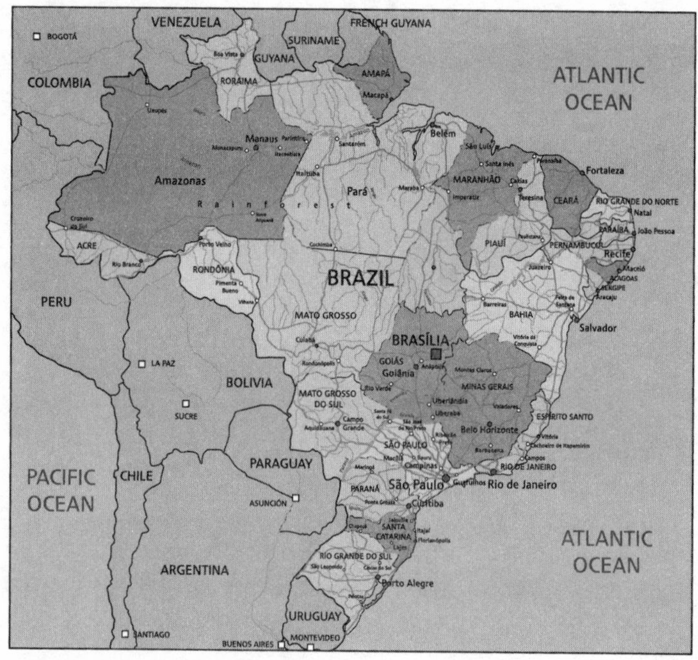

Political Map of Brazil

1

THE COLONIAL AND IMPERIAL PAST

OBSTACLES OR OPPORTUNITIES TO CREATE A MODERN BRAZIL?

Who were the original Brazilians?

When the Portuguese discovered what is today Brazil, they encountered an Amerindian population living along the coast and in the basin of the Paraná and Paraguay Rivers. From early chronicles, the population was linguistically and culturally relatively homogeneous. While there were individual tribes or social groupings, the Portuguese referred to the largest groups of indigenous peoples as the Tupi-Guarani because of their similarity in language and culture. Other smaller groups were interspersed along the coast. From the beginning of colonization, there was considerable prejudice against the Brazilian Indians; to some degree, this continues today.

This was a shocking collision of two very distinct cultures. The Portuguese were at the height of their power. They were unable to understand, we gather, the dramatic difference between a relatively sophisticated European culture of the 16th century and a culture that relied on hunting, fishing, gathering fruit, and raising crops. We do not have accurate data on the number of indigenous peoples living in Brazil in the early

1500s—the estimates range from two to five million people. Today, there are fewer than 300,000 Indians in all of Brazil.

For the Tupi-Guarani, the arrival of the Portuguese was a disaster. Since there was not one Indian nation, the colonizers tried to "divide and conquer." Those villages that supported colonization were favored, the others were not. There was often fierce resistance by the Indian population to the efforts of the Portuguese to enslave them or to convert them to Roman Catholicism. Many fled their traditional homelands to seek survival deeper inland or in the Amazon jungle. The local populations were decimated by epidemics, violence, and repression.

The contrast with the Spanish conquest's resistance could not be greater. The magnificent empires of the Aztecs in today's Mexico and the Incas in Peru and along the Pacific coast of South America were highly organized, and had developed very efficient modes of agriculture and transportation. They were wealthy and proud indigenous societies. But they succumbed to the prowess of the Spanish in dividing and conquering. In both Portuguese and Spanish America, the Indian populations both feared the colonizers and attempted to resist them. But, for the time, overwhelming weaponry, prejudice, and shock opened the native societies to conquest and enslavement.

Why did Spain and Portugal adopt different strategies in colonizing Latin America? What became known as Latin America was an afterthought in the global explorations of Spain and Portugal. The discovery of the "New World" by Christopher Columbus in 1492 opened challenging new opportunities for both countries but it was Spain that profited first and foremost. The discovery of the Inca and Aztec empires in Mexico and in the Andean mountain range of South America yielded immediate wealth. The "sword and the cross"—the conquering invaders or *conquistadores* and the Roman Catholic Church—were the drivers of Spanish American colonization. There were large and sophisticated civilizations to subjugate and govern; indeed, the Indian population was quickly enslaved for Spanish enrichment at the cost of destroying two ancient civilizations. Two viceroyalties were established in 1535—New Spain (Mexico and Central America)—and Peru was established in 1543. Two additional units were created in the 18th century. Spain quickly established authoritarian governing structures in the New World that guaranteed the economic and political interests of the Spanish Empire.

In contrast, Portugal's "discovery" of its portion of the newfound lands was more hesitant and experimental. The new territory (it was not yet clear that South America was a continent, and not an island) represented a small share of the land mass of the continent. The Pope issued the Treaty of Tordesillas in 1494 and drew a line through an imaginary map of the recently discovered lands—Portugal's share was the "hump" of the continent closest to Africa, and Spain received the rest of the South American continent. In 1500, a fleet of thirteen ships left Lisbon bound for India. Blown off course and carried westward by winds and currents in the South Atlantic, the caravan touched down in Pôrto Seguro in the state of Bahia, in the Brazilian northeast. In contrast to Spain's discoveries of highly advanced native societies, Pedro Álvares Cabral and his colleagues encountered naked Indians, the Tupi, who were hunter-gatherers. After eight days, Cabral's flotilla continued to India, sending word back to Portugal of the new discovery. Other fleets followed and relations with the Tupi were slowly established.

After the initial phase of exploration, the royal government decided it needed a plan to manage and exploit the new territory. Portugal, an early seafaring nation, had experimented with different administrative schemes in Africa and the islands of the Atlantic in the 1400s. The decision was made in Lisbon to exploit the new colony with a system of trading factories, and unlike the Spanish New World where gold and other valuable metals were found, the new Portuguese colony offered little more than dyewood (pau Brasil), monkeys, and parrots. Brazil was leased to a small group of merchants in Lisbon; however, once it became clear that it was not a particularly successful venture, the Crown retook control in 1506.

Geopolitics soon became an issue for Lisbon. Spanish explorers were moving south into the area that is now Argentina; French pirating and poaching were emerging as potential threats to the integrity of the colony. A century later, Brazil would still be susceptible to external threats. In 1624 the Dutch West India Company employed its naval and military might to seize Salvador, Bahia but was repulsed soon after. However, Brazil remained a target and the Dutch returned this time to occupy much of the northeast from 1630 to 1654. A Brazilian expedition in the early 1530s established a royal colony in São Vicente (São Paulo). As the possibilities in Brazil began to be better understood in Lisbon, the Crown decided to establish a number of settlements along the coast. A poor kingdom, Portugal decided to entrust the new territories to private investors. Twelve grantees with close connections to the Royal Court were granted donations and they were appointed as captains and governors. The new overseers were expected to produce a steady income stream through trade and development for the government in Lisbon. However, the donations had a mixed record and the Crown once again took ownership of the territories in 1534. Having experimented with commercial concessions and territorial grants, the government decided it was time to send a royal governor to Brazil. Tomé de Sousa (1549–1553) was charged with protecting the former donations from Indian attack and increasing revenues for the royal treasury.

Were social relations with the indigenous populations different under Spanish and Portuguese rule?

The native folk in Spanish America were dominated and subjugated quickly; the King of Spain symbolically replaced the leaders of the Aztec and the Inca empires. But in the case of Brazil, the Tupi did not have an advanced system of government or social organization. Tribal conflict and warfare were frequent. In the first years of settlement, relations with the Indians were relatively distant but cordial. But with the decision to create a royal colony, Lisbon decided to "take charge." This meant a strategy for economic development and a policy for the Indian population. For the first issue, the discovery that the coastal lands were well suited to the cultivation of sugar, a commodity in increasing demand in 16th-century Europe, offered an important source of wealth. For the second, Lisbon chose a newly founded religious order, the Jesuits, to pacify and convert the local indigenous population to Catholicism. The first priests arrived with Tomé de Sousa.

The two goals were contradictory, as it became apparent very quickly. The Jesuits decided to remove the Indians from their villages and resettle them in small communities or *aldeias* to deepen the process of conversion—whether the Tupi wanted to be uprooted or not. As sugar planting spread across the region, the absence of labor became a critical challenge. Indians in the *aldeias* were not available for labor on the plantations, since they were under Jesuit protection. The great debate about enslaving the Indians thus began. Rebellious Indians were candidates for enslavement; passive *aldeia* Indians received royal protection. As the northeast sugar plantations expanded, they encroached on the tribal territories of the Indians, who violently resisted. More and more Indians were classified as rebellious and therefore eligible to be enslaved. But of greater concern to the planters was the fact that the Indians were not farmers; in tribal society, women did that work, not the men. Hence an alternative source of labor was desperately needed.

By mid-century, as more colonizers arrived, disease struck the Indian population, decimating it by large numbers. As H. B. Johnson has commented, "... epidemic disease, enslavement and religious proselytization by the well-meaning Jesuits effectively shattered the defeated Indian culture and societies, leaving the survivors to be reintegrated into a colonial society structured on Portuguese terms."[1]

Were African slaves better treated in Brazil than in the United States?

With the growing demand for labor and the failure to train the Tupi as plantation workers, Portugal turned to the African slave trade to provide the manpower needed on the plantations. The country had been involved in the trade for some time, given its long reach into Africa in the preceding century. As one commentator has said, "the image of a Portuguese colonial legacy of racial tolerance is tantamount to an official ideology, at least within the former colonial power."[2] This sentiment was incorporated into the Brazilian interpretation of slavery. Gilberto Freyre, an American-educated sociologist, was a principal defender and interpreter of this thesis. He argued in his seminal book *Casa Grande e Senzala* (in English titled *The Masters and the Slaves*) that the Portuguese were relatively benign in their treatment of the slaves imported forcefully from Africa. As noted by Anthony W. Marx, the prevailing interpretation of Portuguese colonization was that it was more benign than that of the Spanish. He argues that given the different cultures and traditions encountered in Brazil, the colonizers were more willing to accept the indigenous way of life in comparison to the Spanish. This mythology was widely believed to be true by the ruling elites for a long period of time. The reality, of course, was totally different. A Portuguese priest wrote the following in 1627: "a sugar mill is hell and all the masters of them are damned."[3] A contemporary analyst offered the following analysis: "Time and time again observers who witnessed the roaring furnaces, the boiling cauldrons, the glistening black bodies and the internal whirling of the mill during the 24-hour day of the sugar *safra*, or harvest, used the same image of hell."[4]

While the historical record is fragmented, there appears to be a consensus today that the plight of the African Brazilian population did not change very much after the independence of Brazil in 1822. Large plantations and export crops remained the backbone of the newly independent Brazil. Slave imports continued well into the middle of the 19th century. Brazil came under increasing pressure from the British—who took up the issue of the abolition of slavery in the 1850s.

A major turning point came with the decision to seek European immigrants to work on the newly established coffee plantation in the Paraíba Valley, in central Brazil. While succeeding administrations had begun to respond to British—and international—pressure to end the importation of slavery, the question arose as to why freed slaves—or those still enslaved—were not deemed suitable for work on the plantations. The answer is a simple if difficult one—racism. Racist thought, then prominent in some intellectual circles in Europe, influenced the Brazilian elites that "whitening" Brazil was a reasonable goal. And, from the point of view of the elites, people of color or mixed blood were considered inferior and probably unable to meet the demands of coffee cultivation and export.

After the abolition of slavery in 1888, and a sharp increase in European immigration, the Afro-Brazilian population remained marginalized, uneducated, and with few opportunities of employment other than menial jobs in the growing urban centers or on the plantations where they had been enslaved.

People of color were deliberately excluded from upwardly mobile positions. As Brian P. Owensby has written:

> Blacks and mulattos of all shades confronted great resistance from employers [in the 20th century], they rarely landed jobs in the commercial sector because appearance mattered, and good appearance was something "people of color could not have," as one employer noted. The greatest opportunities for those of darker skins to move out of manual labor were in government employment, where nevertheless most worked as orderlies, doormen, and messengers, not the kinds of jobs likely to vault them into respectability.[5]

The *boa aparência* (good appearance) could still be found in newspaper ads as late as the 1960s. While the situation has improved, perhaps, at the margins of Brazilian society, the data is clear. Illiteracy among nonwhites is far higher than that of whites. Nonwhites are far behind the white population in having completed the compulsory eight years of elementary schooling. Whites in Brazil have a far greater probability than do nonwhites of completing college-level studies. We will return to the very important topic of race relations in contemporary Brazil at the end of the volume.

Why was colonial Brazil, compared to Spanish America, so underdeveloped?

Portuguese oversight of Brazil, given the realities of geography and limited royal resources, was relatively benign, compared to Spain and its colonies. There was never a large military presence in the colony. Education was limited to the very small elite and the Jesuits were responsible for primary and secondary education. But driven by a new, centralizing regime in Lisbon, the Jesuits were seen as an obstacle to new policies that would turn Indians from tribesmen to peasants. The "sanctuaries" established by the Jesuits were seen as outdated and often a challenge to the needs of local elites for labor. When the Jesuits were expelled in 1759, educational opportunities were greatly reduced. There were no universities in Brazil and those seeking higher education had to return to Europe. Printing presses were not allowed. Trade was strongly tied to the motherland.

The colonial economy focused on cycles in which one crop was dominant and then replaced by another. Sugar was dominant for well over a century, with smaller cotton, tobacco, and cacao cycles. The *senhores de engenho* (the owners of the large plantations) were conspicuous consumers of imported luxury goods but apparently less committed to investments in new technologies. By the early 17th century, Brazil was the world's leading sugar producer and exporter. But by the end of the century the export boom had faded. Brazil faced increasing production and productivity from the British, Dutch, and French colonies. The sugar plantations did not disappear, but slowly went into decline, relegating the northeast region to centuries of neglect and underdevelopment.

The second important cycle was the discovery of gold in the 1690s in what is now the state of Minas Gerais, in the center of the country. A gold rush ensued. For the first time since the discovery, there was a large influx of Portuguese drawn to the colony with the prospects of rapid enrichment. The mines flourished for about a century. One important outcome of the gold rush was the emergence of Rio de Janeiro as the major port for the exportation of the mining wealth. The city emerged as an important financial and services center. As the city grew, the Portuguese government decided to move the capital of the colony from Salvador, Bahia to Rio in 1763.

As the mines became exhausted, the mining population dispersed. Some became cattle ranchers, and others moved into agricultural production. By the end of the 18th century, Brazil stagnated, as did Portugal. The latter suffered a number of reverses. A massive earthquake destroyed the capital city, Lisbon, in November 1755. The government had been involved in two costly wars with Spain over competing claims to territory in South America. One of the major sources of income for the Crown had been the revenues from the gold and diamond mines but, as noted, productivity declined precipitously in the late 1700s. Portugal had depended on the income from Brazil to cover a constant trade deficit with the rest of the world. Under the chief minister, the Marquis of Pombal, efforts were made to stimulate the Brazilian economy but they came to a halt with his fall from power in March 1777, following the death of King José I. Pombal and his supporters did attempt to centralize administrative authority in the colony. The province of Grão Pará and Maranhão, a separate state since 1621, was integrated into the now consolidated Brazilian state in 1774. Brazil now was governed by one viceroy. But given overlapping jurisdictions with local provincial administrators, many of whom responded directly to Lisbon, the viceroy, based in Rio de Janeiro, had limited authority. Many writers have noted that the efforts to resuscitate the economy were hamstrung by terrible transportation, inadequate ports, and low levels of entrepreneurship given the lack of an educated, mobile entrepreneurial class.

Importantly, 1750 was the year that the Treaty of Madrid was signed. It recognized the steady expansion of the colony from a relatively small portion of the South American continent to one-half of that land mass. Soon after settlement, official expeditions began exploring the inland territory via the Amazon River and its tributaries. Out of São Vicente in the south, private expeditions of *bandeirantes* (from the Portuguese word for banners or flags), beginning in the 1580s, moved into the interior in search of Indian captives and mineral wealth. Inexorably, the boundaries of the colony moved westward into what had been considered Spanish territory by the Treaty of Tordesillas. There were no roads or means of transportation over the Andean mountains. In effect, there were two South Americas, the one facing the Pacific Ocean and the other on the Atlantic coast. There was little communication between them for centuries.

The Andean mountain range and inhospitable terrain in general made it almost impossible for the Spanish-American authorities in Lima and other administrative centers to thwart the "creation" of modern Brazil. Spain and Portugal agreed in the negotiations to abandon the basic principle of Tordesillas. With the Treaty, Brazil now occupied about one-half of the continent and almost the entire Amazon.

The final years of the colony witnessed signs of political upheaval. The first was a conspiracy organized in Ouro Preto in the province of Minas Gerais in 1788–1789. Minas Gerais—or the "General Mines"—was a source of great wealth for the Portuguese monarchy. It was an inland province that appeared to have greater intellectual ferment than in other parts of the colony. The wealth from the mines appeared to provide an impetus for a large number of local Brazilians to leave Brazil to be educated in Europe, since there was no university in the colony. They returned imbued with new ideas about politics and society.

Their aim was to establish a *mineiro* republic. The plot was discovered; the conspirators were arrested; some were exiled to Angola; one was hanged. A second conspiracy was discovered in Bahia in 1798. The rebels wanted to establish a French-style republic. They too were apprehended and punished. In 1807 another plot was uncovered and suppressed, also in Bahia. The final conspiracy coincided with the demand by Napoleon Bonaparte that Portugal close its ports to British ships, detain British subjects, and seize their property. Great Britain had been Portugal's strongest ally for a number of decades. In response to the threat from Napoleon, the British government sent a fleet to warn Lisbon that it must not comply. The British government offered to escort the government to Brazil. As a French army approached Lisbon, the government of the Regent, Prince Dom João, the de facto ruler of Portugal and its colonial possessions, agreed. On November 29, 1807, thousands of courtiers and members of the royal family set sail for Brazil. They arrived in Salvador, Bahia in January 1808; two months later, the royal court was installed in Rio de Janeiro.

Was the arrival of the Braganza Dynasty in 1808 a positive or negative development for Brazil?

The arrival of the royal family, not a decision taken in Brazil, needs to be placed in context. By the end of the 18th century, there began to emerge a sense of "being Brazilian" in the colony. Members of the elite traveled abroad with some frequency. Some were educated at universities in Coimbra, Montpellier, Edinburgh, and Paris. Despite the somewhat frantic efforts of the Board of Censorship in Lisbon, books were smuggled into Brazil from Europe and North America.

Voices were raised in the colony regarding the long-term relationship—economic and political—with the mother country. The ideas of the French Revolution and the upheaval in Haiti circulated and were debated. There was open hostility between the Portuguese and those who were Brazilian-born. But the ties between the colony and the colonial power were far more benign than between the native-born people in Spanish America and Madrid. Given the relative weakness of the Portuguese state, and the vast territory that was now formally recognized as Brazil, imperial power was diluted. Brazilian planters and merchants had relatively fluid linkages to European metropolitan merchants. As exporters of agricultural goods, the ties were significant. Brazil was also dependent on Lisbon for the continued import of African slaves, given the absence of a native work force.

As many have noted, the arrival of the court in Brazil was the first time a reigning European monarch had traveled to the New World. Rio de Janeiro was now the de facto capital of the empire. While still in Bahia, the Prince Regent had opened Brazil's ports to all trading nations, ending imperial control. Great Britain would become a major beneficiary of this decision. Rio de Janeiro became the center of British trade with not only Brazil but all of South America. The Regent had little choice in the matter. He was dependent on the British to protect Portugal from the French and on the British fleet to defend Brazil and the other components of the empire.

Brazil began to change dramatically after 1808. The first printing press was established and books and newspapers appeared for the first time. Libraries and literary associations flourished. New people and new ideas were part of the changing colony. Naturalists, scientists, artists, and travelers were welcome. Brazil's flora and fauna, its geography and natural resources, and its Indian population, fascinated Europe and North America. The population of Rio de Janeiro doubled from 50,000 to 100,000 during the residency of Dom João.

With the defeat of Napoleon and the liberation of Portugal, plans were made for the return of the Prince Regent and the court to Lisbon. The British sent a small flotilla to Rio de Janeiro to escort him home. Dom João equivocated; he was enjoying his time in Brazil. He finally decided to remain and raised the colony to the status of kingdom—equal to Portugal. Unlike Spanish America, where Napoleon took the royal family captive, Brazil was now the center of an empire. There was no crisis of political legitimacy since the King was in Brazil (he had succeeded to the throne on the death of his mother).

But differences began to appear. The cost of supporting the royal entourage fell on Brazilian shoulders. It became clear that the court was as interested in pursuing Portuguese interests as in nurturing those of Brazil. With little local consultation, Dom João ordered troops to the Rio de la Plata (Argentina) in 1816; the Portuguese occupied Montevideo in 1817 in an effort to secure the southern border of the colony. The Anglo-Portuguese commercial treaty appeared to favor the motherland over the colony. British pressure on Lisbon to halt the slave trade threatened the economic interests of the landed elite. At the Congress of Vienna in 1815, Portugal agreed to ban the slave trade north of the equator in return for a financial indemnity. In 1817, Portugal gave the British fleet the right to stop and search ships on the high seas suspected of illegal slaving north of the equator. To Brazil, this was a vital interest; Portugal was seen as nonsupportive. In March 1817, there was a revolt in the northeast; the British refused to recognize the "republic of the northeast" and it quickly collapsed.

In August 1820, a liberal-nationalist rebellion began in Oporto (Portugal), followed by another in Lisbon. Portugal felt abandoned. The liberals demanded the return of the King. The primary motivation, though, on the part of the Portuguese elites, was to restore Brazil to the status of a colony. Brazil was divided. Many members of the court wanted to return to Europe; others had settled in Brazil and saw little advantage to returning. Brazilians feared that the economic and social improvements that occurred after the arrival of the royal court might be jeopardized by a new Parliament that was driving the demand for the return of the King. Finally, in April 1821 Dom João set sail for Portugal, leaving his son, Pedro, in Rio de Janeiro as Prince Regent.

Elections for deputies to the new Parliament were held across the empire. As the Brazilian deputies began to arrive in Lisbon, the Parliament acted to reduce Brazil to its former status. Finally, in October, the Prince Regent was ordered to return home. Refusing to swear loyalty to the newly promulgated 1822 Constitution, the Brazilian delegates returned to Brazil. The Portuguese and the Brazilian factions now squared off. Brazilians withdrew their allegiance to Dom João and transferred it to Dom Pedro. Pressure grew on the Regent to decide his course of action; on January 9, 1822 he declared that he would remain in Brazil. In an important symbolic gesture, a wealthy Brazilian, José Bonifácio de Andrada e Silva, was appointed the head of a new "Brazilian" cabinet. José Bonifácio became the leading decision maker; he was progressive on social issues but profoundly conservative on political affairs. He saw the monarchy as a critical institution if there was to be a transition from colony to independent state.

In June of that year, Dom Pedro agreed to call a Constituent Assembly, to be elected indirectly with very limited suffrage. In this way, José Bonifácio hoped to neutralize the liberals and radicals. On September 7, 1822, Dom Pedro received instructions from Lisbon—his decrees were to be revoked and his ministers charged with treason. In a fit of anger, he declared "Long live independence, liberty, and the separation of Brazil." In October he was acclaimed Constitutional Emperor and Perpetual Defender of Brazil. He was crowned on December

1, 1822 in Rio de Janeiro. However, strong pockets of support for Portugal persisted, especially in the provinces of the northeast. Could Brazil remain united? Dom Pedro, in desperation, turned to a mercenary and former British naval officer, Lord Cochrane. He organized a Brazilian naval squadron to break the Portuguese hold on Bahia. The Portuguese forces fled and a Brazilian army entered Salvador, restoring Brazilian control. The reaction against the Portuguese presence had been driven by the economic interests and social concerns of the *senhores de engenho* who opposed recolonization. The victory over the Portuguese, in favor of a united Brazil, was viewed as a conservative victory for the established elite interests in the country. Cochrane and his compatriots successfully ejected the remaining Portuguese forces and the last contingent left Brazil in March of 1824.

With Brazil independent, it was critical to have diplomatic recognition granted by the powers of the day. Great Britain, given its long-standing relationship with Brazil, was the first to be approached by the government. Brazil was now Britain's third-largest foreign market. In the eyes of the Foreign Office in London, the fact that the monarchy had been preserved was a dominant consideration. The rulers of Britain were not favorably inclined to the spread of republican democracy. Most important, London hoped to link diplomatic recognition with the abolition of the slave trade. Britain had become the leading nation to condemn the trade and urge its abolition in very strong language. This was a complicated situation since the bedrock support for the Brazilian empire rested with the plantation owners; they had no alternative source of labor other than slavery.

The issue of recognition of Brazil by Portugal was a daunting policy challenge as well. Britain agreed to mediate relations between the new empire and the former mother country. As these deliberations moved forward, the United States became the first country to recognize Brazil's independence on May 26, 1824. A British emissary was dispatched to Rio de Janeiro in

July 1825 and within a few weeks was able to secure a treaty by which Portugal recognized the independence of Brazil. Recognition by Britain followed, as did a treaty in November 1826 by which the Brazilian slave trade would be declared illegal three years following the ratification of the document. Especially important for London, an Anglo-Brazilian commercial treaty was signed in August 1827, giving Britain a privileged position in access to the Brazilian market.

By the end of the 1820s, Brazilian independence was relatively secure. The transition from colony to empire had been reasonably peaceful. Brazil had achieved the important diplomatic recognition from Britain and, thereby, a guarantee that Portugal would offer no serious opposition to the new relationship. Dom Pedro was viewed by the elites as an important symbol of social stability and national unity. The governmental structure installed by Dom João in 1808 continued to function. Liberal and radical forces had been neutralized and a conservative regime now governed, with little opposition, in Rio de Janeiro.

The arrival of the Braganza dynasty in Brazil in 1808 was, in general, a positive development. Dom João opened the country to trade and commercial opportunities never imagined by the colony, and his return to Portugal allowed the dynasty to continue in the person of Dom Pedro. Institutional continuity was important in the transition from colony to independent empire. Brazil fortunately could rely on the strong financial and diplomatic support of a world power, Great Britain. While the abolition of slavery remained a delicate and challenging issue for the new nation-state, it would require decades of discussion and diplomacy before abolition finally was achieved in 1888.

Did the Brazilian Empire (1822–1889) hinder or help the modernization process?

While the political transition was generally peaceful, the empire began life with many disadvantages. A small population—perhaps 4 or 5 million—was spread across half a continent. Rather than an integrated nation-state, the country resembled a loosely connected series of provinces, often with little in common. It is fair to say that there was little sense of national identity or economic unity. The country was still profoundly rural and woefully undereducated. It is estimated that less than one-third of the population was white. The great majority was black or mulatto and the slave population was probably one-third of that. While Brazil was no longer the largest producer of sugar, that crop remained very important and represented about 40 percent of the country's export earnings. Cotton, coffee, cacao, hides, and tobacco followed. As noted before, Britain was Brazil's major banker and commercial partner. The bulk of the manufactured goods imported into Brazil were produced in Britain.

Politically, the empire faced a number of challenges. A matter of debate among the political elite was whether Dom Pedro was really Brazilian or whether he remained a Portuguese prince "in hiding." At the time of the treaty by which Portugal recognized the independence of Brazil, Dom Pedro retained the right to succeed to the throne of Portugal. From 1822 until his abdication in April 1831, Dom Pedro remained a controversial figure. The first challenging issue to be addressed by the Constituent Assembly that met in May 1823 was about the role and powers of the Emperor. It was widely believed that Pedro favored absolutist rule. The Assembly was deeply divided and the Emperor abruptly and forcibly dissolved it. Dom Pedro created a Council of State that proceeded to draft a new constitution that was announced in March 1824. It was a document that concentrated power in the hands of the Emperor. He appointed the ministers and the provincial presidents. The franchise was very restricted. The document gave the Emperor a "moderating power" to allow him to dissolve the Chamber and call new elections. He had veto power over legislation and the constitution confirmed the Council of State, the members of which were appointed for life by the Emperor.

Violent protests against the autocratic outcome of the constitutional process erupted, all of which were quickly put down. Dom Pedro was viewed as very close to the Portuguese community in Rio de Janeiro and apparently less so with the new "Brazilian" elite. Some expressed concern that at the death of his father he would exercise his right to return to Portugal to assume the throne—would Brazil then be relegated to colonial status once again? In general, however, the monarchy in the early years of the empire remained popular, but that popularity waned as the decade ended. Economic factors were not in favor of the government. The prices of many of the country's exports fell in the 1820s, and the Anglo-Brazilian commercial treaty increasingly appeared to be a straitjacket, with great benefits for the British but few for the Brazilians. The 15 percent limit on tariffs on British goods curtailed government income, and the money supply increased by 10 percent per year from 1822 to 1829.

Urban discontent became a challenge at the end of the decade. While expectations had been high for a better standard of living in 1822, it proved not to be true. Frustration grew, often aimed at the Portuguese merchants and, ultimately, at the Emperor. A crisis erupted in April 1831 with noisy and often violent protests in Rio de Janeiro. The military turned against the Emperor and sought to rid the army of Portuguese officers. On April 7 of that year, the Emperor abdicated the throne and boarded a British warship to return to Portugal, where he died in September 1834. His five-year-old son was proclaimed emperor along with a three-man regency to guide the empire until he came of age. A period of unrest across the country ensued after the abdication. Various political factions expressed their opinion in street demonstrations and protests—liberals and radicals, absolutists, a few republicans, and those favoring a return to rule by Portugal. In response to the unrest and the ongoing unpopularity of the army, a National Guard was established in 1831. It became an important national institution charged with keeping order, protecting public buildings, and precluding any lower-class agitation.

As was probably inevitable in a highly unequal society, the Guard quickly fell under the influence of local powerbrokers across the country.

A series of regional revolts erupted in the early 1830s. While the empire itself was not threatened, a military response was required in most instances. The political elites, divided over what sort of government was needed and possible, realigned, and two political parties were created: the Conservative Party and the Liberal Party. They would dominate national politics until the fall of the empire in 1889. In response to ongoing uncertainty about the political future of the country, the fifteen-year-old emperor was prematurely installed on July 23, 1840. The government continued in the hands of senior politicians for some years to come.

The 1830s and 1840s witnessed the appearance of the next and most important economic cycle in the province of Rio de Janeiro. Coffee would become the stabilizing factor in the Brazilian economy as demand in Europe and the United States grew steadily. Cultivation expanded into the Paraíba Valley and parts of Minas Gerais and São Paulo. By the mid-1830s, coffee was king; it was the principal export and revenue producer (and it would remain so for more than a century). As the demand for labor on the coffee *fazendas* grew dramatically, slavery became a front-and-center issue. Brazilian governments were unable to implement the British antislave trade law of 1831, bringing the British and the Brazilians into conflict. Further complicating the situation, law enforcement was not national; it rested in the hands of municipal and provincial officials. Illegal slave shipments continued and were overlooked by local authorities, often members or close friends of the planter aristocracy.

The slave trade was significantly impacted by the actions of the British. In response to growing and increasingly aggressive action by the British fleet to stop the slave trade in the Atlantic, Brazilian political elites for the first time began to consider alternative sources of labor. Some in the elite realized that, in the longer run, slavery would not be a viable option. Given the certainty of African slaves, little thought had been given to immigration in the preceding centuries. But the realization that Brazil was moving against history began to spread. This was made even more urgent when the British government passed the Slave Trade (Brazil) Act in August 1845, which authorized the navy to treat Brazilian slave ships as pirate vessels; they could then be subjected for condemnation before British vice-admiralty courts. But the trade actually increased, became better organized, and was highly profitable. Apparently, a majority of senior policymakers in Rio de Janeiro continued to support the slave trade. In 1850, the British added additional ships and manpower to the coast of Brazil to implement the 1845 law. In the same year, the British government also instructed British warships that they could enter Brazilian territorial waters and even the ports of Brazil.

Why was it so difficult to create an integrated, unified Brazil, and why did the empire collapse?

The empire was dominated by a small group of social, economic, and political elites. The vast majority of the population—whether of color, Indian, or poor freedmen—did not participate in any way in decision making either at the local or the national level. The population was concentrated along the eastern seaboard. Rio de Janeiro, São Paulo, and Minas Gerais dominated the empire. Wealth and social status were enjoyed by a very small segment of the population. Land ownership was highly concentrated. Little attention was given to physical infrastructure, further emphasizing regionalism and further impeding national integration.

As the empire consolidated, foreign policy became increasingly relevant. While Brazil had survived earlier efforts of separatist movements, Spanish America had fragmented. Uruguay was created in 1828 as a buffer state between Argentina and Brazil. The Viceroyalty of the River Plate did not survive the wars of independence early in the 19th century. After years of conflict, new nation-states emerged—Argentina, Uruguay, Paraguay, and Bolivia. Borders were porous and issues of navigation and trade on the Paraguay River grew in importance. The dictator of Paraguay, Francisco Solano López, decided to assert Paraguay's sovereignty on the river. His naval forces seized a Brazilian ship in November 1864.

His neighbors viewed Solano Lopez as a bully and interloper in the confusing geopolitics of the Southern Cone. In May 1865, the governments of Argentina, Brazil, and Uruguay signed the Treaty of the Triple Alliance. The Argentines led the conflict in its early phase; the Brazilians in the final years of the conflict. Brazilian troops entered the Paraguayan capital, Asunción, in January 1869. Solano Lopez was surrounded and killed. The population of Paraguay had been decimated by the war; most of the survivors were old people, women, and children. Brazil would continue to have a large influence in the country for decades to come.

The war had created the first "modern" Brazilian army. A new generation of officers was created to lead the troops. Enlisted men consisted of members of the regular army and the National Guard. But former slaves, and in some cases those still held in slavery, were sent to fight. A new esprit de corps emerged as the military blamed the politicians at home for the length of the war, for shortages of supplies, poor equipment, and, seemingly, little respect for the efforts of the fighting forces. Out of the war emerged a newly unified armed force seeking change in Brazilian politics and society.

One question was the appropriate role of the National Guard. Another was the position of mid-level officers in the army who were not linked to the wealthy supporters of the Guard or to the powerful political elites. The Liberal and Conservative parties were divided over war strategy, and after the conflict ended, the enmity deepened regarding a national reform agenda. By the decade following the war with Paraguay, it was apparent that a new generation of reform-minded intellectuals, politicians, businessmen, and progressive planters looked to create a more modern Brazil. They lobbied for the abolition of slavery, favored European immigration, preferred federalism, and believed that church and state should be separated. Many joined the Republican Party, created in December 1870.

By the 1880s, Brazil's population had reached approximately fourteen million. Coffee was clearly the dominant factor in the national economy. The country began to urbanize following the Paraguayan war, and, thanks to coffee profits, urban amenities were possible—paved roads, streetcars, and the telegraph were signs of a new Brazil. Railroads were finally a reality, beginning the process of integrating the internal market. For the first time, albeit slowly, light manufacturing appeared. Education, while not a high priority, did develop in the cities. Political change was inevitable. The oligarchical structure of the early empire was seen as anachronistic. Electoral fraud, which had been the practice, was less acceptable. The working class in the cities began to emerge as an important source of votes and, indeed, had its own agenda. Conflicts between the civilian politicians and the armed forces grew, as the latter believed the former were not supportive of military modernization. Bitterness spread over the attempts of the political elite to influence military promotions. Reformist priests resented the control of the church by the government.

The old system of patronage politics began to appear antiquated, often hindering talented individuals who, without elite links, were overlooked in public service. The lack of a professional civil service meant that bureaucratic decisions were based on personalism and favoritism.

As the empire was ending, abolition became a controversial issue. In 1871, a bill was approved in Parliament supporting the emancipation of newborn children of slaves. The law of free birth was the beginning of a wave of reforms in the final decades of the empire. Military salaries were increased and the system of promotion was made more transparent. A voter certificate was created, reducing electoral fraud. The vote was extended to non-Catholics, freedmen, and naturalized foreigners. Indirect elections were abolished. The two parties of the empire were often divided on the content and the pace of reform, requiring the Emperor to use his moderating power frequently.

In 1884, slavery was abolished in the provinces of Ceará and Amazonas. Manumissions (the freeing of slaves by their owners), long part of the complicated institution of slavery, grew dramatically. On May 13, 1888, the Parliament approved a law abolishing slavery without compensation. In the absence of Dom Pedro, his daughter signed the "Golden Law." Conflict between the army and the regime escalated. The Republicans saw a unique opportunity and lobbied the high command to overthrow the empire, which occurred on November 15, 1889, and a Republic was proclaimed. Dom Pedro and his family quietly left Brazil for exile in Europe. In hindsight, the monarchy was doomed by the 1880s. New social forces had emerged that had little interest in the trappings of the throne. The economy was modernizing, the idea of a republic was appealing—and the continuation of patronage politics was not. The aging Emperor, while respected, was no longer revered. The military would now become a major force in national politics and continue to be so well into the middle of the next century.

2

FROM THE REPUBLIC TO THE *ESTADO NOVO*

Did the creation of the Republic contribute to the modernization of Brazil?

The overthrow of the empire redefined the political contours of Brazil. The two traditional parties of the empire imploded and were replaced with a national Republican Party. Decentralization of political power became a reality with a great deal of decision making transferred to the states (the old provinces) and the counties. Power relationships were fluid across the country. The state presidents—or governors—were the powerbrokers between the local political bosses and the state oligarchies, and between the state oligarchies and the federal government in Rio de Janeiro. It was a system characterized by widespread clientelism and patronage. São Paulo and Minas Gerais came to dominate the federation in an arrangement where local/provincial autonomy was recognized *de facto* and in return, provincial delegations were sent to the Parliament in Rio de Janeiro that supported the policies of the two powerful states. Presidents, with few exceptions, came from the two dominant states. An important role of the Parliament was to support policies that protected the coffee industry, the dominant export crop, and the driver of federal finances.

While textile factories had begun to emerge in the last decades of the empire, there was little in the way of industry.

Textiles were followed by the domestic production of clothing, shoes, and food—all light industries. Some analysts have argued that World War I represented a turning point in industrial expansion. But Werner Baer, an American economist who specializes in Brazil, has correctly pointed out that "World War I was not a catalyst to industrial growth, principally because the interruption of shipping made it difficult to import the capital goods necessary to increase production capacity, and within Brazil no capital goods industry existed at the time."[1]

Coffee's share of exports rose from 56 percent in 1919 to more than 75 percent in 1924.[2] It was only in the years following World War I that heavy industry began to emerge. Small steel plants and capital goods enterprises led the way. The production of domestic cement began in the 1920s. Some foreign investment entered the country in the same period and the federal government initiated policies—tax exemptions and guaranteed interest loans—to support new firms. There was also the challenge to domestic industry of the inflow of cheaper and better quality foreign products. But the country remained mainly agricultural in orientation and mentality.

After two military presidents following the fall of the empire, politics reverted to civilian political elites. In eleven presidential elections, nine of the presidents were from São Paulo and three from Minas Gerais. The Constitution of 1891 expanded political participation and the vote was extended to all literate males. The electorate began to increase incrementally, primarily in the cities. But the Republic was also traumatized by a series of rural rebellions that began in the late 1890s and did not end entirely until after the First World War. Many of these rebellions were based on religious beliefs, disaffection, and rural marginalization. For the urban elites in the southeast of the country, these events were deeply disturbing. Great efforts were made after the creation of the Republic to promote the image of an increasingly modern and sophisticated Brazil. World news coverage of these rebellions ran counter to the efforts of the elite to redefine the image of Brazil to the world. Social banditry was not uncommon in the backlands of the northeast well into the 1930s.

The 1920s were the beginning of the end of the Republic—but it would take the decade to produce the institutional crisis that would see it collapse. While São Paulo (SP) and Minas Gerais (MG) were the powerbrokers in the decades following the establishment of the Republic, the southern state of Rio Grande do Sul (RGS), adjacent to Argentina, emerged as a key player in national politics following the First World War. RGS joined Minas Gerais to support a military candidate in the 1910 presidential election over the candidate of São Paulo. This represented the reentry of the armed forces into national politics and the rise of the State of Rio Grande do Sul to national prominence. The state's congressional delegation in Rio de Janeiro began to seek out like-minded representatives to either neutralize or challenge the policy initiatives of the two major players, the states of Minas Gerais and São Paulo. It was also important that many "gauchos" (residents of Rio Grande do Sul) entered military careers; this proved a natural "bridge" to the military high command.

There was growing resentment among the smaller states of the federation with the de facto veto power the two big states held over national policy. There was also a concern that the coffee-generated wealth of the state of São Paulo placed other states at a disadvantage in national affairs. The emergence of RGS was seen as a meaningful alternative to the excessive influence of the two major states in national policymaking.

Politics in the 1920s became more contentious. In the presidential race of 1922, RGS vehemently opposed the São Paulo–Minas Gerais candidate. The RGS leadership saw it as a continuation of a wasteful and expensive policy of support for the coffee powerbrokers. In 1926, a Democratic Party (PD) was established in São Paulo, openly challenging the authoritarian grip on politics by the national Republican Party. The PD became the party of a new generation of business people, intellectuals, lawyers, and students.

In the armed forces, rebellion was in the air. In 1922, a group of middle-rank officers (*tenentes*) openly challenged the status quo and, in July 1922, organized a protest movement in Rio at Fort Copacabana. It failed but quickly became a rallying cry for those who favored institutional change. In 1924, a rebellion took place in São Paulo; in October of that year new protests erupted in RGS. The "columns" joined forces and began a long journey through the interior hoping to arouse the population in the backlands—without success. It moved across the border into Bolivia in February 1927. But the "Prestes Column" (named for its most famous military leader, Luís Carlos Prestes) was now part of the political life of the Republic. A better-educated military generation, the *tenentes* often broke with their commanders over the appropriate role of the armed forces in society. It was a nationalist movement that wanted institutional reform, fiscal probity, and a reduction of the influence in national life of the coffee barons and their acolytes.

The early 1920s also saw a flourishing of Brazilian art and literature. The Modern Art Week (*Semana de Arte Moderna*) opened in São Paulo in February 1922. Organized by Emiliano Di Cavalcanti, a well-known painter, and poet Mario de Andrade, it introduced modernism to Brazilian society—in contrast with the European orientation that had dominated Brazilian art and writing for decades. It consisted of plastic arts exhibitions, lectures, and concerts. It was controversial and colorful. Following the event, various groups emerged to represent often divergent interpretations of the Brazilian reality. The Week opened a long debate over the quality and value of domestically inspired culture in contrast to that imported from abroad.

A calm before the storm characterized the middle years of the 1920s. RGS, seeking greater national influence, agreed to endorse the candidate of the states of São Paulo and Minas Gerais. In return, Getúlio Vargas, a rising star in the politics of RGS, was appointed federal Finance Minister. The preelectoral maneuvering for the 1930 presidential election began early.

Tradition called for a politician from Minas Gerais to succeed the incumbent chief executive from São Paulo. Tradition was overturned and President Washington Luís agreed to nominate another São Paulo politician as the chief presidential candidate.

Feeling betrayed, the president of Minas Gerais province gained the support of RGS; the new alliance nominated Getúlio Vargas, the former Finance Minister, who had returned home to become governor. The Liberal Alliance, as the challenger ticket was called, indicated as vice president a leader from a small state in the northeast, for regional balance. The Alliance appeared to gain substantial support from emerging urban groups, students, and non-coffee-related elites.

The Alliance called for policies to protect workers, attacked the coffee support policies of the past, and called for economic diversification. To gain the support of the *tenentes* (the young military officers who rebelled throughout the 1920s against corruption, the influence of São Paulo, and military unpreparedness), Vargas called for transparent political reform, amnesty, and the rights of the individual. Vargas, of course, lost the election of March 1, 1930. But in the aftermath of the defeat, the Alliance blossomed. Younger politicians in SP, MG, and RGS wanted an opportunity to rise and replace senior leaders. The younger military officers continued to pressure for military modernization and clean politics. A conspiracy had begun. Bringing together disparate elements in national life, the rebellion began on October 3, 1930 in RGS, and the next day in the northeast. Employing the old "moderating power," the high command of the military intervened on October 24 and deposed the president. After a brief military junta, Getúlio Vargas was installed in the presidential palace on November 3, 1930.

The Republic was a painful and combative period in Brazilian history—economically, politically, and culturally. Economically, coffee and coffee supports squeezed out opportunities for diversification. The Republic concentrated resources in one export crop to the disadvantage of other possible economic opportunities. It made the state of São Paulo the dominant economic and political force in the country. In political terms, the Republic was a continuation of the regional and oligarchic politics of the empire. While it decentralized political power to the states and municipalities, it did not enlarge the franchise or sufficiently address deep-seated problems of poverty and inequality. The former slave population was abandoned. While foreign immigration provided a much needed new work force, its members were not seen as "Brazilian."

Because of its failures, the Republic inexorably fostered opposition. The young *tenentes* were the first new leadership option since the fall of the empire in 1889. They openly challenged the cozy relationship between the aging military leadership and the coffee elites of São Paulo. The Week of Modern Art signaled that the cultural values of the Republic, imported from abroad, were outdated. The emergence of the Democratic Party in São Paulo demonstrated that a more modern Brazil was seeking its "voice." And the rise of RGS, and individuals like Getúlio Vargas, indicated that the old order had to adapt or disappear. It disappeared in October 1930. Could the Republic have been different? It is difficult to say given the realities of 1889, but it is probably the case that the odds were very small that the institutional continuities of the transition and the establishment of the Republic could have been more inclusive and democratic.

Was 1930 the real beginning of the 20th century for Brazil?

The Vargas era opened in the context of the world depression of 1929. As one analyst has succinctly stated:

> The depression of the 1930s had a severely negative impact on Brazil's exports, whose value fell from US$445.9 million in 1929 to US$180.6 million in 1932. The price of coffee in 1931 was at one-third of the average price in the years

> 1925–1929 and the country's terms of trade had fallen by fifty percent. In addition to the decline in export receipts, the entrance of foreign capital had almost come to a complete halt by 1932.[3]

The government was forced to take a number of drastic measures in an attempt to stabilize the economy. A major challenge was the country's foreign debt obligations. In August 1931 it suspended part of scheduled debt payments and opened talks to reach a debt consolidation agreement. The regime also introduced exchange and other direct controls. The currency was devalued as well. The critical concern of the Vargas government was to protect the coffee sector, the principal source of foreign exchange. The National Coffee Council was created in May 1931, transferring the coffee support program from the state of São Paulo to the federal government. The Council was empowered to buy all of the coffee available and to destroy the crop that could not be sold or stored. Measures were also taken to support the indebted coffee growers.

Vargas's political challenge was the delicate task of coordinating a diverse political coalition. The principal actors were the dissident military officers that had forced President Washington Luís to resign; the *tenentes*, who were divided; the liberal constitutionalists represented by the Democratic Party; an emerging urban middle class; ironically, the coffee planters who were upset by the policies of the Luís government that had maintained a fixed exchange rate that reduced their income as the price of coffee fell on the international market; and the political "outs" across the country who felt ignored by the powerful federal government in Rio de Janeiro.

Vargas—or "Getúlio" as he is usually called, a tradition in Brazilian society—moved quickly to consolidate his grip on national power. On November 11 he became the "Chief of the Provisional Government" with both executive and legislative authority. All legislative bodies at all levels were closed. The government created the post of "Interventor" to replace the sitting state governors. The principal difference in the coalition was over the question of how quickly national elections should be scheduled. The "democrats" wanted immediate elections; the *tenentes* argued for the postponement of any election, fearing that the traditional oligarchies would mobilize the voters to support a return to a version of the *status quo ante*.

Getúlio emerged as a master manipulator by appearing to support both groups. But under growing pressure, the government announced a new electoral code. That drove the *tenentes* to pressure Getúlio to repudiate the calls for a Constitutent Assembly. Other challenges included a growing rebellion in São Paulo against the new government in Rio de Janeiro that was viewed as an interloper in the internal affairs of the coffee republic. And in RGS, opposition grew over Getúlio's equivocating with the *tenentes*—refusing to commit himself to a more authoritarian form of government. The first outright challenge to the new government came on July 9, 1932, when an armed revolt began in São Paulo. The expectation among the Paulista rebels was that other states would join in the struggle for liberal constitutional reforms. But that demand became mixed with calls for regional autonomy among some of the Paulista rebels and other states refused to commit to support that goal. Getúlio was helped by the fact that major *ancien regime* figures in RGS and Minas Gerais favored support for the rebels; they were arrested and the threat from the Old Republic oligarchy disappeared. Getúlio cultivated a new generation of political leaders across the country and was able to politically isolate São Paulo. A military offensive under the direction of a staunch Getúlio ally, General Góes Monteiro, blocked the Paulista forces from moving against Rio de Janeiro. Other state forces entered São Paulo and finally, after a two-month siege, the rebels surrendered.

To bring the country together, elections for the Constituent Assembly were held on May 3, 1933 in what were perhaps the first honest elections in Brazilian history. The Assembly drafted a new Constitution that came into force in mid-1934, providing a legal framework for the new government. Getúlio was elected president in July 1934 by the Chamber of Deputies for a term that would end with direct national elections in January 1938.

In many ways, 1930 did introduce Brazil to the 20th century. The powerful oligarchies of the Old Republic, while not destroyed, were weakened, and space was opened for new, modern political leaders. The inefficient decentralization of the pre-1930 years was ended and a stronger, more authoritative regime emerged in Rio de Janeiro. Coffee interests, while critical to the economic future of Brazil, lost their political veto over national politics. One discordant note was the rise of the influence of the armed forces in national politics once again. They had ended the empire and the Old Republic and would now play a central role for decades to come.

Why did Brazilian democracy collapse in the 1930s?

Getúlio Vargas became president of Brazil in a moment of international geopolitical uncertainty that began to be mirrored at home. Democratic representative political parties were never part of the Brazilian DNA and that was proven once again in the 1930s. Reflecting the growing polarization in Europe, Brazil's political process divided into two opposing groups, one heavily influenced by the Communist Party, and led by the charismatic Luís Carlos Prestes of *tenentes* fame—the National Liberation Alliance (ANL or *Aliança Nacional Libertadora*). The right was embodied in a fascist-inspired movement, Integralism, led by a swaggering figure named Plínio Salgado. These well-organized and financed groups quickly overwhelmed the remnants of the 1930 Liberal Alliance and came to dominate the streets. Getúlio was in his element. He carefully turned one against the other and created the impression among the average Brazilian citizen that open, competitive politics was both a luxury—and dangerous.

Left-wing groups committed political suicide when they organized a barracks revolt in the northeast in November 1935 and murdered a number of senior military officers. A minor revolt in Rio de Janeiro was easily contained. Quickly, Getúlio requested a state of siege from the Congress that was approved. The National Security Law, passed in March of that year, was amended to give the president extraordinary powers. The Alliance was closed, its leaders arrested, and thousands of followers—military and civilian—were detained. The Integralists were the only remaining viable political movement.

Planning began for the 1938 elections. Getúlio could not succeed himself under the 1934 Constitution. Two principal candidates quickly emerged, one a former governor of the state of São Paulo who represented the liberal constitutionalist groups in society, the other a populist *tenente* from the impoverished northeast. Conspicuously, Getúlio chose not to endorse either candidate. Within the Getúlio camp, it became clear that they should urge him to "take charge" and retain power for the good of the nation. To strengthen his hand with a potential "veto" player, the military, Getúlio nominated General Góes Monteiro as Army Chief of Staff. Another stalwart supporter of the president, General Eurico Dutra, became War Minister. To strengthen his grip on national politics, new loyal Interventors were assigned to a number of states to neutralize any interference in Getúlio's plans. Conveniently, General Góes Monteiro's staff "uncovered" documentation purporting to lay out plans for a Communist Party–led revolution. Dutra conveniently denounced the plot; Congress approved the suspension of constitutional rights. On November 10 the national Congress was closed and in a radio address to the nation that day, Getúlio stated that Brazil could not entertain the "democracy of parties" which "threatens national unity."[4] A new authoritarian constitution was quickly promulgated, modeled on the fascist and corporatist documents then *de rigeur* in Europe. Political parties were abolished on December 2 and would not reappear until 1944. The *Estado Novo* (New State—EN) became the new political reality in Brazil.

There is no doubt that Getúlio's personal ambition to retain power drove the dynamics of the 1930s. He cleverly outwitted the left and would do so very soon with the right. He won over senior military officers who feared further advances by the radical left. The urban middle class was confused and frightened. They clearly wanted to avoid a political outcome that could resemble Nazi Germany, Mussolini's Italy, or Stalin's Soviet Union. Both the left wing and the right wing were seen as undemocratic and prone to violence and repression. Local politicians understood the new realities of power and acquiesced quickly to the new order.

Did the Estado Novo *make any positive contributions to Brazilian development?*

Getúlio's "New State" was a soft authoritarian adventure. It was not violent but it was repressive. However large numbers of people did not disappear. Grudging acceptance was all that was expected by the authorities in Rio de Janeiro. The president quickly moved to further centralize and modernize the federal government. Powers once exercised by the states and counties were transferred to the federal administration. As early as November 1930 a new Ministry of Labor, Industry, and Commerce had been created. Federal ownership of railways and shipping and mixed public-private companies were created under the aegis of Rio de Janeiro. Social welfare programs were centralized. The taxing powers of the states were sharply reduced. In response to the new federal programs, the national bureaucracy expanded rapidly. This also opened patronage opportunities for the regime. Slowly but surely the once all-powerful state political oligarchies were sidelined. As the Second World War appeared to have turned the tide against the fascists, Getúlio sensed that political change at home would become popular. He targeted the working class as a probable prime source of future political support. Social welfare programs were instituted. A new union structure was organized, but tightly controlled by the Ministry of Labor—paternalism at work. Getúlio began to emerge as the "Father of the Poor."

There were important innovations in the national economy as well. Coffee remained the dominant export crop in the 1930s but the government began to experiment with industrial policies to reduce the republic's dependence on one crop. Rio de Janeiro began a program of investments in infrastructure, basic industries such as oil and steel, and increased public investment in projects deemed able to diversify the economy. A national steel company—Volta Redonda—was created in 1941. Brazil's formal entry into World War Two in 1942 led to a rigorous policy of economic mobilization to produce the raw materials and manufactured goods that would be needed for the war effort. For the first time in the country's history, industrialization became a matter of national interest—and urgency. Brazil was about to challenge the empire of coffee.

The New State of Getúlio Vargas did contribute to the modernization of Brazil in a number of ways. It created a set of national institutions. It began to see the need to reduce the country's dependence on coffee exports. It created a rationale for industrialization. It decided to support the Allies in World War Two on the side of the democratic forces. But the New State, ironically, remained highly undemocratic at home. The central government determined and controlled the ebb and flow of political activities until 1944. In repressing democratic dialogue and participation, it would make the transition to a democratic regime more complicated.

World War II: What was the relationship between the United States and Brazil?

As commented earlier, the United States was the first country to recognize Brazil's independence in 1824. Brazil was the first country to recognize the 1823 Monroe Doctrine (aimed at excluding European powers from the region). Dom Pedro II made a successful visit to the United States in 1876. An "unwritten alliance" emerged at the end of the 19th century with the establishment of the Republic. Brazil began to shift its diplomatic focus from London to Washington, DC. Much of the impetus for this new relationship was driven, in the early years of the 20th century, by the Foreign Minister of Brazil, the Baron of Rio Branco. The economic complementarity between the two nations strengthened the alliance. In 1905, both countries increased diplomatic intercourse by raising their missions to the status of embassies in 1905. Brazil formally entered the First World War in October 1917 in support of the Western alliance. After the war, the United States increased its trade relationship with Brazil and over the ensuring years, it would replace Europe as Brazil's major partner. The election of Franklin Delano Roosevelt in 1932 opened an opportunity for renewed US interest in Latin America through the "Good Neighbor" policy announced in March 1933. In March 1940, the United States approved a $25 million loan to support the development of Volta Redonda.

The turning point in deepening the relations between Rio de Janeiro and Washington, DC was 1941. Conversations between the two countries had begun in the late 1930s regarding cooperation in case of war. As Britta Crandall has written,

> the 1,800 mile distance between Africa and the "Brazilian bulge" of Brazil's Northeast was seen as the most practical and probable route of any Axis invasion. While this type of European aggression may seem improbable in hindsight, in mid-1940 the fear of a Nazi push through Africa and across the South Atlantic Ocean to Brazil was a genuine concern, especially if Great Britain were defeated. And with no land defenses, Brazil was incredibly vulnerable to any large-scale invasion or air attack.[5]

The northeast of Brazil was viewed by the Roosevelt administration as critical to US defense strategy in the Caribbean and the rest of the continent. Many in Washington feared fascist regimes in Europe inspiring right-wing uprisings in South America. Getúlio saw an opening to the United States as a way of replacing the now nonexistent trade with Germany. The United States, from his viewpoint, could be critical in supplying the Brazilian armed forces with much needed armaments and training. Brazil agreed to provide 100 percent of its strategic materials—rubber, iron, cotton, etc.—to the United States at noncompetitive prices. A secret treaty in May 1942 gave the United States permission to build military bases in the northeast, a major breakthrough for Allied strategy. The air base in the city of Natal quickly became the center of Allied air traffic. After Pearl Harbor in December 1941, Getúlio opened all Brazilian ports and airfields to US forces.

Brazil declared war on Germany and Italy on August 22, 1942. The Roosevelt administration sought to deepen the bilateral ties by sending a technical aid mission to Brazil in 1942. As the relationship matured, the Brazilian government decided to commit troops to the war effort. The Brazilian Expeditionary Force (FEB) went to Europe in 1944. Brazil benefited handsomely from the American Lend-Lease program and received more military equipment than any other country in the region. As a symbol of the relationship, President Roosevelt stopped in Brazil in January 1943, on his return from a summit in Casablanca, to meet with Getúlio. The relationship was strongly supported by the ambassadors of each country and the respective foreign ministers. Both capitals came to see the relationship as a win-win situation. While relations were cordial prior to the war, they became deep and mutually reinforcing during the conflict. The death of FDR in April 1945 and the succession of Vice President Harry Truman—combined with the end of the war and a change in White House, Pentagon, and State Department personnel—removed Brazil from the high priority list in Washington, DC. The Cold War in Europe was about to begin. The hemisphere was viewed as marginal in that effort.

Was the end of the New State a "given" at the end of World War II?

Getúlio understood the delicacy of the moment once it appeared that the war was winding down with the total defeat of the Axis powers. The contrast between young Brazilians fighting to restore democracy in Europe and the continuation of the New State at home was obvious. In November 1943 and again in April 1944, the president made veiled references to restoring democratic government at home—at some time in the future. The year 1945 saw the first public signs of opposition to the continuation of the New State—and of Getúlio as head of state. An amendment to the 1937 Constitution was issued in February stating that a decree would be issued within ninety days setting a date for elections.

The first opposition candidate emerged and he represented the first new political party. Former *tenente* Major General Eduardo Gomes of the Air Force was chosen to represent the liberal constitutionalists on the ticket of the Democratic National Union (UDN). Getúlio equivocated, openly defending the 1937 Constitution in comments in March 1945. Public protests broke out across the country and on March 11, Getúlio announced that he would not be a candidate in the elections. Suddenly, the War Minister, General Dutra, was proposed as a candidate. The question was whether or not he was an "official" candidate, actually representing Getúlio, as opposed to an independent candidate. The momentum had begun to shift to ending the New State. The government released long-held political prisoners including Luís Carlos Prestes, who took the leadership of the recently legalized Communist Party; Dutra accepted the nomination of another new party, the Social Democratic Party (PSD), that had been established in May. The promised decree appeared on May 28; the election date was set for December 2, 1945.

Suddenly Vargas supporters vehemently campaigned to postpone the presidential election but agreed to hold elections for the Constituent Assembly. It was obvious—if the Assembly met under the Vargas presidency, Getúlio would have a great deal of say in its content. A third new political party was organized to support Getúlio—the Brazilian Labor Party (PTB). Getúlio appeared undisturbed by the increasing political tumult. But in October, the president spoke to a large demonstration that had gathered in front of the palace and commented that he was not a candidate but the people had the right to demand a Constituent Assembly. Shortly thereafter, the government unexpectedly changed the election rules. The national election date was set for December 2, 1945. State and local elections were to be held after the December 2 balloting.

The decree required incumbent officeholders who were seeking to be elected to resign; they would be replaced, of course, by government appointees, loyal to Getúlio and thus able to influence the election outcome. Recklessly, Getúlio removed the police chief of the federal district and appointed his brother, an unsavory character in local political life. The police chief notified the War Minister, who notified General Dutra; an agreement was quickly reached among the senior commanders that they would give Getúlio an ultimatum—withdraw his brother's nomination or be removed by the army. Getúlio refused. It was too late. Another senior officer, and long-standing friend, told the president that the army was determined to end his mandate. On October 30 he left Rio de Janeiro for RGS and political exile. Once again, the "moderating power" was exercised by the armed forces, not the civilian leadership. The military made it clear that they indeed held the power to disrupt the constitutional process in defense of the nation. Getúlio could probably have avoided pressure from civil society to resign; he understood the realities of military politics too well to resist.

3

THE "EXPERIMENT" IN DEMOCRACY, 1945–1964

WHY DID IT FAIL?

Thomas Skidmore, in his definitive book on Brazil titled *Politics in Brazil, 1930–1964: An Experiment in Democracy,* wrote that "all Brazilians, regardless of political position, seem agreed that April 1, 1964, was a watershed in postwar Brazilian history."[1] This section of the book will identify the principal "fault lines" of the period from 1945 to 1964. The military, having ended Getúlio's fifteen years in power, overshadowed the establishment of the next republican experiment. They would also terminate the government in power in 1964 and install a twenty-one-year-long "authoritarian-bureaucratic state."

The 1945–1946 transition

The two principal candidates in the presidential elections were military veterans of the 1930–1945 period. General Góes Monteiro resigned as War Minister in the interim government but was "persuaded" by colleagues to accept the position of "Commander in Chief of the Army." The interim authorities revoked many of Getúlio's last decrees and confirmed the election date of December 2. The newest players in the political process were the new political parties. They soon became victims of the disputes and controversies of the past fifteen years. The PSD (Social Democratic Party), neither social nor democratic in orientation, was an umbrella for the fans of Getúlio—bureaucrats, industrialists, large landowners, bankers, and, the most recent recruit, the growing urban working class favored by Getúlio in the New State. A small segment of the working class, who were organized in a new union structure, opted for the PTB (Brazilian Workers Party). A significant number of urban voters favored the recently legalized Communist Party. The UDN (Democratic National Union) received the support of small- and medium-sized businesses, some middle-class military officers, the liberal constitutionalists of the 1930s, and others hoping the party would stand up to the corruption and cronyism of the past fifteen years.

Against tradition, the December 2, 1945 elections were viewed as relatively transparent and clean. Dutra carried the day with 55 percent of the national vote, carrying the large key states; Gomes and the UDN received 35 percent of the vote. Save for a brief moment in the early 1960s, the UDN would be relegated to the margins of Brazilian politics thereafter. The Communist Party candidate received 10 percent of the vote. General Dutra became president in January 1946. The newly elected Congress, whose seats were spread across a number of parties, with the PSD in the lead, also met as a Constituent Assembly to draft a new constitution. Promulgated in 1946, it excluded illiterates and enlisted men in the military from voting.

Dutra: A forgotten president?

The Dutra years saw a return to partisan party squabbling. Getúlio, elected a federal senator on the PSD ticket in RGS, broke with Dutra and urged workers to join the Workers Party. Post–1945, the Communist Party (PCB), again legal, resumed activity. The PCB began to take a more forceful and negative position in Congress and across the country. The PCB stood against the old ways of Brazilian politics; that was appealing to many urban voters who were looking for new leaders and new policies. The party made strong headway in infiltrating the unions. In 1947 local elections, it consolidated its position as the fourth largest party in the country. Invoking an "anti-democratic parties" clause in the new constitution, Dutra declared the PCB illegal in 1947—just as the Cold War opened. The government suppressed left-wing labor leaders and many of their supporters. The PTB quickly moved into the political space lost by the PCB.

Getúlio was clearly plotting a return to power. He supported PTB candidates in the 1947 elections for Congress and PSD aspirants for state office. Post–1946 witnessed a new type of player in national politics: populist politicians who, linked formally to one of the established parties, reached out beyond to appeal to a wider popular constituency. The program of post–1946 populist politicians combined the use of the media, patronage, theatrics on the campaign stump, and "handouts" for the poor. Getúlio had his sights on the next presidential election in October 1950 and assumed the role of a populist candidate.

On the economic front, Brazil emerged from World War II with an export structure similar to that of the previous decades—coffee, cacao, cotton, sugar, and tobacco. But there was a growing sense among the decision-making elite that it was time to embrace industrialization with enthusiasm. This position was supported by the realization that the prices for Brazil's exports were volatile and pricing took place in world commodity markets. It was apparent that the country's share of that world market was declining. According to the newly established Economic Commission for Latin America (ECLA) in Santiago, Chile, countries like Brazil were on the "periphery" of the world economy, and consumers and industrial countries were at the "center."

Brazil had emerged from the war with significant foreign exchange reserves that disappeared in a year's time, given an import buying spree. In reaction to that reality, policymakers resorted to foreign exchange controls from 1947 to 1953.

Foreign exchange—usually US dollars—was made available according to a five-category system of priorities determined by the Export-Import Department of the Bank of Brazil. Essential goods, such as medicines, insecticides, and fertilizers, were allowed to be freely imported. The importing of consumer goods was discouraged but priority was given to essential foodstuffs, cement, paper and printing equipment, and machinery. The government's new economic development plan called for the replacement of a wide array of imports; these goods would now be domestically produced under Import Substitution Industrialization (ISI). The priority items were seen as essential to the implementation of the new program.

Was the return of Getúlio Vargas inevitable?

The 1950 national campaign opened during this heated debate over the economic future of Brazil. Cleverly Getúlio had decided that he could combine the electoral strength of the PSD and the PTB as the road back to the presidential palace. Getúlio was updating the New State for a new political era. Moving away from the corporatist institutional framework of the 1930s, he now saw an opportunity to reinvent himself as the champion of social welfare reform, the spokesman for the working class, and a promoter of economic nationalism.

To assure his nomination and ultimate victory, Getúlio needed to neutralize potential opposition. The military was first and foremost. In a sophisticated maneuver, he reached out to General Góes Monteiro who assured him that the military would not object to his return to the palace as long as he respected the Constitution and did not threaten the prerogatives of the armed forces. His next challenge was the populist governor of São Paulo, Adhemar de Barros, who had built a formidable political machine—the Progressive Social Party (*Partido Social Progressista* or PSP). Adhemar had presidential ambitions but understood it was probably too early to seek the presidency. On June 7, 1950, Getúlio accepted the nomination of both the PTB and the PSP for the October 3, 1950 election.

The PSD, nominally Getúlio's party, was nonplussed. At President Dutra's insistence, the party nominated a little-known lawyer from Minas Gerais to carry the flag for the PSD. But Getúlio used his formidable skills to reach out to many of the "old guard" in the PSD to "neutralize" their support for the Dutra candidate and to quietly support the PTB/PSP ticket. The UDN, unable to identify a joint candidate with the PSD, launched their own nominee. Getúlio stressed the need to deepen the industrial process, popularly called "developmentalism." Campaigning across the country, Getúlio left the opposition candidates in the dust and carried 48.7 percent of the vote.

In the context of a new, fledgling political party system, the weight of personality won out in the 1950 election. Getúlio Vargas was fondly remembered by many, but not all, Brazilians. He personified Brazil's "coming of age." His commitment to welfare programs won over those less fortunate. Compared to his two lackluster opponents, he offered a new vision for a modern Brazil. The stars were aligned in Getúlio's favor in 1950. But that state of affairs would not last very long.

Was Getúlio Vargas his own worst enemy after his reelection?

Taking office on January 31, 1951, Getúlio Vargas seemed not to understand how different Brazil was even from 1945. Industrialization and urbanization, beginning in the 1940s, was transforming the nation. The urban working class had grown considerably as a result of the expansion of industry. A burgeoning urban middle class had become consumers. And the latter was and would continue to be an important political force in national politics. Brian P. Owensby nicely captures the ephemeral nature of this "new" middle class:

> These people lived as much by their yearnings and fantasies as by objective reality. They faced lives of possibility defined by markets, sifting hierarchies, the potential for mobility, and certain imagined political relationships that allowed a wide array of people to take up middle-class roles in explicit and implicit comparison with others.[2]

The overwhelming fear of the new middle class was the fear of falling into a lower social category of people of color with manual or menial employment. Since it was almost impossible to "rise" in Brazil in the 1950s, the middle class was insecure and desperate for leadership that would consolidate their social and economic status. The inability of increasingly polarized elites to do this—primarily through the control of inflation—would prove a turning point in the collapse of the Republic in 1964.

Getúlio's return to the presidential residence in the Catete section of Rio de Janeiro coincided with a growing debate over the appropriate—and possible—course of development. Thomas Skidmore identified three broad approaches to the challenge—neoliberal, developmentalist-nationalist, and radical-nationalist.[3] The first school was orthodox in their approach to national finances. Balanced budgets and tight control over the money supply were key, as was a welcome role for foreign capital. The second group's approach was often traced to the early program of the *tenentes*. Industrialization was an imperative and a mixed-economy model (market-oriented capitalism with a heavy dose of government intervention and control) was viewed as necessary. An enhanced role for the state was important to break bottlenecks and open investment strategies in areas where the private sector was not yet ready or prepared to do so. The third approach saw a vast conspiracy to hold Brazil back from its rightful place in the world order. Capitalists and foreign investors wanted to "exploit" Brazil.

The radical nationalists were, apparently, less interested in a coherent program of economic growth and industrialization and much more devoted to upending the existing political and social order. While the weakest of the three in 1951, they would steal the show in the 1960s and play an important and disastrous role in the military coup of 1964.

As always, a major constraint on any development strategy was the perennial problem of the balance of payments. The country needed increased foreign exchange earnings to import inputs required for industry, but commodity exports would not reduce that bottleneck. Borrowing abroad was one solution that would become part of the economic mix over the next decade. As Getúlio took office, inflation became a major concern of policymakers for the next decade

It is not clear that Getúlio Vargas either understood the various options available to his government in the economic and financial field, or sought first and foremost to maintain the upper hand politically. The latter appears to be more accurate as he resumed the presidency. Getúlio was, and always had been, a poker player but a modest risk taker. He understood the need to maintain an international image as a prudent president while, simultaneously, he understood the need to control inflation and assuage the fears of the middle class. As a result of a report of a Joint Brazil–United States Economic Development Commission, the government decided to establish a National Bank for Economic Development (*Banco Nacional de Desenvolvimento Econômico*, or *BNDE*).The Finance Minister announced a five-year plan that allotted $1 billion in investments in basic industries. It became clear that the old system of exchange controls and the overvalued currency were obstacles to growth and the system was reorganized in January 1953.

Getúlio held a relatively benign view of foreign investment when he returned to Catete in 1951 but over the next year his rhetoric began to highlight the "exploitation" of Brazil by foreign interests. He opted for state corporations as a major vehicle for national investment strategies. The first byproduct in October 1953 was the organization of a public-private petroleum corporation—Petrobras—with a majority of the shares held by the government. But the decision to create Petrobras opened a polemical national debate as to the direction of the economy. The PCB, reflecting Cold War passions, took the lead in attempting to outflank Getúlio in defending the economic independence of Brazil. As always, Getúlio left the polemics to others. Sensing that there was general support for Petrobras, he proposed to create Electrobras (the national electricity company) for similar reasons. Getúlio's nationalism deepened and he took aim at foreign companies in Brazil expatriating profits abroad. In January 1952, a decree was issued limiting remittances to 10 percent of a company's annual earnings. But he was careful to send a message that in general the country benefitted from FDI.

The political situation began to deteriorate soon after his inauguration. The right wing was historically opposed to anything that Getúlio Vargas supported. The UDN became the principal advocate of destabilizing the Vargas regime whenever possible. Some efforts were made to incorporate the UDN in the government but the high level of hostility made that impossible. It became apparent that the right wing saw Getúlio's return to power as a violation of the liberal constitutionalist movement of the 1930s and 1940s. He was not to be trusted. There was something inherently wrong with a democratic system that would allow Getúlio to return to power. Some younger military officers shared the views of the UDN. While the high command had sanctioned Getúlio's inauguration, he was well aware that times had changed and that he had to continually win the endorsement of the military leaders. But as fate would have it, global developments became part of the debate over the role of the armed forces in national life.

The Cold War began to divide the armed forces, as some opted for a more nationalist position and even identified with the rhetoric of the PCB, reflecting the Moscow line of propaganda. Others in the officer corps looked with concern on this polarization. What position should Brazil adopt in the Cold War? The issue of foreign capital became a new "hot" topic for the officer corps. It appeared as though national political tensions over the Cold War were being played out in the influential Military Club, located in Rio de Janeiro. Elections for the governing board of the Military Club pitted moderate officers, who usually backed closer ties with the United States, against those who supported a more anti-American, pro-Brazil foreign Policy.

Elections for the Directorate soon became a sort of "plebiscite" on whether the moderates would dominate the debate. In crucial elections on May 21, 1952, the two camps went to battle and the moderates won by a large majority. This provided Getúlio needed breathing space as he turned to a variety of other pressing policy challenges.

In the context of a highly politicized campaign of economic nationalism, inflation began to exacerbate social tensions in Brazil. The government appeared unable to contain the constant increase in prices; the need to adjust wages and salaries began to polarize the country. The group most affected was the "new" urban working class. While the Dutra government had been able to contain discontent, the Vargas government catered to more aggressive leaders of the labor movement and they began to lobby for wage adjustments. The traditional export class remained dubious about the economic program of the government. The middle class, frightened as always, began to question what their economic and social future would be. A radical element emerged in national politics that argued for far-reaching reforms, redistribution of wealth and, ultimately, a dramatic shift in relations among social classes.

Jockeying for political space, Getúlio reorganized the cabinet in the summer of 1953. Some old reliable figures were brought back to power; but new younger players emerged. The Goulart appointment signaled that Getúlio was turning to the PTB and the left wing to consolidate his base—and to insure that he would control the succession to the presidency in 1955. Goulart, or "Jango" as he was known, represented a possibly dangerous turn of events. Viewed as leftist in orientation, the unions, emerging as spokesmen for the industrialization process, were not shy in championing their demands. This threatened the middle class. It also alarmed the more nationalist, right-wing military officers. Industrial leaders were nonplussed—where did Getúlio really stand on the issue of national development and democratic governance?

The government finally announced an anti-inflation campaign in October 1953. Very tight credit control became the backbone of the plan. The balance-of-payments deficit was addressed with new exchange controls that the government hoped would make exports cheaper overseas and make imports more expensive. But then an unexpected development raised concerns in Rio de Janeiro: the advent of the Eisenhower administration in January 1953. Economic orthodoxy was the preferred policy of economic development. Foreign countries were expected to provide a warm welcome for foreign direct investors. It was also decided to begin to phase out promised financing for projects developed by a joint United States–Brazil Economic Commission. Washington's shift in approach to development—after a more benign policy under the Harry Truman administration—came as a shock and provided grist for the radical-nationalist mill. The United States was obviously opposed to Brazil's modernization; the US government supported those who sought to exploit countries on the periphery, like Brazil.

Inexorably, the long-suffering middle class felt that no one was really interested in their concerns. But suddenly, an unexpected "spokesman" emerged. Jânio Quadros, a relative unknown in the state of São Paulo, ran and defeated the traditional parties to become mayor of the City of São Paulo. His appeal for votes was directed at the middle class. He played on the growing fear of rising inflation. He called for "clean" government and a chance for the "little man." Quietly, the

Quadros phenomenon identified another social sector increasingly concerned over the course of national affairs—the military. Many of the officer class were of middle-class origin. This group eschewed the radical nationalism of some in the officer corps. Nor were they persuaded by the far right. They began to seek a middle ground for a strategy of national development that would increase and distribute resources in a framework of constitutional legality.

Getúlio appeared to drift further to the left in 1954. In January he accused foreign firms of taking illegal profits out of Brazil. The cost of living continued to rise and public demonstrations pressured the government "to do something." A debate opened in Rio de Janeiro about the need to increase the minimum wage—but by how much and what would be too much? And it would fall to the Minister of Labor, Jango, to recommend to Getúlio the appropriate amount of the increase.

Slowly, Brazilian politics appeared to be spinning out of control. The anti-Getúlio press became more indignant with what they saw as misuse of public power. Conservative military circles were concerned over Brazil's position regarding the Cold War. In February 1954 a group of mid-rank military officers wrote a letter to the War Minister protesting their low salaries. The letter stated that the troops were demoralized; the government had neglected much needed modernization of equipment; and officers were leaving the corps to work in the civilian sector. Moreover, there was concern over whether or not the yet-to-be announced minimum wage increase would further marginalize military family income. The issue of status in post–1946 Brazil was never far from the surface and the surge of the working class appeared to be beginning to unhinge the officer corps—could a working man earn more than a military officer? On February 22, 1954, Jango announced his recommendation: a 100-percent increase in the minimum wage, which applied mostly to the urban commercial and industrial workers. Jango resigned that day as well.

Getúlio waited until May 1, the international socialist holiday, to announce his decision: a 100-percent increase in the minimum wage. The country erupted with criticism from every quarter—except the urban workers! As expected, the wage increase proved to be inflationary. The balance of payments had not improved. And coffee prices fell precipitately on world markets. Getúlio might have been able to "stare down" his attackers but an assassination attempt against a crusading journalist, Carlos Lacerda, failed but succeeded in killing a colleague, an Air Force major.

This immediately drew the armed forces into the debate. It was soon discovered that the assassin had ties to the presidential guard at the palace. Resignation demands began to circulate, which Getúlio rejected. Vice President Café Filho broke relations with the president. The military once again, as in 1945, insisted on his resignation. He refused. A final military manifesto was issued to the president on August 24. President Vargas then committed suicide, leaving a letter that turned the tide in his favor even in death:

> Once more the forces and interests against the people are newly coordinated and rose against me. They do not accuse me, they insult me; they do not fight me, they slander me and do not give me the right of defense. They need to drown my voice and halt my actions so that I no longer continue to defend, as I have always defended, the people and principally the humble. . . . I fought against the looting of Brazil. I fought against the looting of the people. I have fought bare breasted. The hatred, infamy, and calumny did not beat down my spirit. I gave you my life. Now I offer my death. Nothing remains. Serenely I take the first step on the road to eternity, and I leave life to enter history.[4]

Whether authentic or not, the document set the political tone of the country for the next decade before the collapse of the Republic in 1964. The country was clearly divided between anti-Getúlistas and his supporters. The vice president was sworn in immediately; he chose a relatively moderate cabinet. As scheduled, congressional elections were held on October 3, 1954. There was little change in the party representation. The campaign for the presidential election of October 1955 began immediately after the congressional vote. The PSD quickly nominated Governor Juscelino Kubitschek ("JK") of Minas Gerais. Over anti-Getúlistas protestations, Jango Goulart of the PTB became JK's running mate. The anti-Getúlistas' candidate was a former *tenente* General Juarez Távora. JK took 36 percent of the vote; Távora 30 percent; Adhemar de Barros 26 percent; and Plínio Salgado 8 percent (a plurality was sufficient to be declared the winner). Jango Goulart won the vice presidency with more votes than JK (presidential and vice presidential candidates did not run as a formal "ticket," but as individuals bound together in a loose electoral alliance).

Carlos Lacerda, the target of the failed assassination attempt, led the media attack to prevent the inauguration of JK and Jango. It became clear very quickly that the final word would rest with the armed forces; the War Minister indicated that legality would be followed and the inauguration would take place. Suddenly, on November 8, Vice President João Café Filho was hospitalized and unable to carry out his duties. He was replaced by the president of the Chamber of Deputies. Amidst tense maneuvers to prevent the transfer of power, the former War Minister, General Henrique Lott, deposed the acting president, who was seen as sympathetic to the conspirators who favored canceling the elections. The president of the Senate was sworn in, following the constitutional succession process. Later in 1955, after the election of Juscelino Kubitschek as president, there emerged renewed concerns over military reaction to the democratic election. For this reason, a state of siege was imposed through the inauguration on January 31, 1956 of the new chief executive.

Why was Kubitschek so successful a president given the circumstances of his election?

JK was a career politician with an impressive record as mayor of Belo Horizonte and governor of Minas Gerais. A charismatic figure, he promised Brazil "fifty years of progress in five," and he basically delivered. Industrial investment and production soared. Private investors were welcomed—unequivocally—and given incentives to invest in Brazil. Structural bottlenecks in transportation and power were addressed. Production "targets" were announced and followed. Within a short period of time the pessimism of the early 1950s dissipated, a newfound confidence was apparent throughout the country, and JK was the cheerleader in chief. In one bold stroke, he tried to neutralize the animosities of the previous decade and lead Brazil into the future. The idea of an inland capital had been written into the Constitution of 1891. Debated for many decades, it was usually dismissed as utopian or too costly. Besides, Brazil was a coastal city; its beaches were a major attraction for the public and the site of a new capital, in the middle of nowhere, was not viewed as attractive to the average Brazilian. To the disbelief of the president—and perhaps the Congress—a bill was approved in 1956 to proceed. Kubitschek wasted no time. He hired a world-renowned architect, Oscar Niemeyer, and a famous Brazilian architect, Lucio Costa. It quickly gained popular support and was seen as a major contribution to Brazil's reputation as a country that believed in big projects that would enhance its international profile.

A consummate politician, JK provided equal access to the presidential palace to industrialists, political party brokers, landowners, union leaders, and the administrative elite that governed the country. While the ever moody middle class was pleased with the country's economic progress, they remained fearful of any policy changes that would negatively impact their status and well-being. The military were treated with deference and given ample funding for salaries and supplies. To demonstrate that his government was not a silent sympathizer with the radical left, he followed a very orthodox foreign policy. The building of Brasília also gave the president new forms of patronage for his supporters and many of those still wary of his political credentials.

JK understood that good relations with the United States were in his interest. Following the dramatic visit to Latin America of Vice President Richard Nixon in May 1958, JK proposed "Operation Pan America" to the Eisenhower administration. While not received with enthusiasm immediately in Washington, DC, it was given more importance after January 1, 1959 and the victory of Fidel Castro in Cuba.

Congressional elections held in October 1958 saw no surprises—the same balance of power among the major parties was preserved. The only policy issue that threatened the "fifty years in five" was the return of inflation. The cost of living began to increase. The balance of payments became a difficult issue once again. There was a noticeable deterioration in the country's terms of trade. Suddenly, the "happy" days of the administration appeared under a dark cloud. The government turned to the IMF for advice and for approval of its new anti-inflation program. That endorsement was crucial to facilitate new lines of credit from its foreign bankers and the United States. The year 1959 proved to be one of reckoning for JK. Political opposition increased as the administration moved toward "lame duck" status. The anti-American radical nationalists denounced the negotiations with the IMF. The old arguments were rolled out that Brazil was being exploited by foreign interests. Dramatically, JK broke off negotiations with the IMF in June 1959. The stabilization program of 1958 was put on hold. Cabinet changes were made and those viewed as "sell-outs" to foreign interests were dismissed. As the campaign of 1960 opened, there was a sense of foreboding among the political elite. Not only was the economy overheating but the political discourse was as well. In part this reflected a number of important developments in civil society that emerged in strength during the "fifty years in five" paradigm.

Would the rise of Catholic radicals in the 1950s contribute to the sense of crisis that emerged in the early 1960s?

It has often been observed that the Catholic Church in Brazil was a "poor" church compared to its counterparts in Spanish America. It was also an institution that was usually closely identified with the social and political elites that dominated the country for centuries. But beginning in the 1940s, in response, in part, to developments in Europe, the hierarchy in Brazil decided to subscribe to the concept of a "lay apostolate," Catholic Action. The movement had been supported by a series of popes in the beginning of the 20th century. The emphasis was on energizing all layers of society in the mission of the Church. In Brazil, the key proponent was Dom Sebastião Leme, the Cardinal Archbishop of Rio de Janeiro (1921–1942). Various organizational efforts were undertaken in the 1920s and 1930s but it was not until the 1950s that Catholic Action reorganized and created a number of affiliates: university students (JUC), workers (JOC), secondary school students (JEC), and agrarian youth (JAC). The most important would become the JUC, which was formally launched in 1950.

JUC complemented a renaissance within the hierarchy of the Roman Catholic Church in Brazil in the 1950s and became an important part of the dynamics of the administration of JK. Postwar Brazilian bishops begin to focus on the underdevelopment of the northeast region of the country. By the 1600s the Brazilian economy moved south, first to the mining area of the state of Minas Gerais, and then to the coffee plantations in and around the state of São Paulo. Sugar, the basis of the economy of the northeast, became increasingly marginal as new producers appeared in the Caribbean and elsewhere. The old sugar plantations remained marginally active but were no longer the heart of the export economy. Slowly the regional economy deteriorated, as did the social and economic conditions of the largely Afro-Brazilian population.

Under the leadership of Dom Hélder Câmara, an auxiliary bishop in Rio de Janeiro, the National Conference of Brazilian Bishops (CNBB) was created in 1952. A series of meetings were held in the region to discuss ways in which the Church might address the chronic poverty and lack of education among the rural population. In May 1956 a major conference was held in Campina Grande, Paraíba under the auspices of the CNBB. The meeting lasted six days and was closed by JK. The bishops of the northeast issue a lengthy document following the meeting, which analyzed the socioeconomic situation in the region and called for a coordinated effort by the government to address the endemic problems that had been ignored for centuries. The call for action led to the creation of the Superintendency for the Development of the Northeast (SUDENE) in 1959, with enthusiastic support from the CNBB.

While the CNBB focused on concrete development goals, JUC had begun to explore Brazilian "reality" in both a more theoretical and action-oriented approach. In 1959 JUC formulated the concept of the *ideal histórico,* based on the writings of Jacques Maritain. In part motivated by the progressive nature of the JK government, JUC decided to open a debate about Brazil's future. Documents published by JUC called for the overcoming of underdevelopment; liberating the country from capitalism, viewed as a structural impediment to a national development agenda; and finally the need to restructure the existing international equilibrium that was generated by capitalism.

JUC thinking paralleled that of the National Union of Students (UNE) that was calling for institutional reform at the university level. The debate soon began to question existing political and economic institutions as well as the social class system that remained hierarchical and elite driven, from JUC's perspective. The Catholic hierarchy was not amused by the apparent radical turn that JUC was taking. It appeared to the bishops that JUC was challenging the appropriate role between the bishops and the youth movement. To some in the leadership of the Church, JUC was taking a dangerous step that could lead to an independent movement free of Church supervision.

In June of 1962, Popular Action (AP) was launched as a political movement, not a party, and with a great deal of support from the more radical members of JUC. The movement received intellectual support from the two papal encyclicals of Pope John XXIII issued in the early 1960s and seen as a defense of policies that favored the poor and marginal worldwide. AP moved beyond the *ideal histórico* and replaced it with a new concept, *consciência histórica*—historical consciousness. The new concept looked to history to understand what needed to be transformed through action. AP and its followers also developed the theory of *conscientização*—the raising of the people's consciousness before radical transformation could take place. The theory was put to practice through mass literacy programs and an emphasis on "popular" culture. At the same time in the northeast city of Recife, an educator named Paulo Freire had devised a method of mass literacy programs for the poor. Many of these threads came together in March 1961 when the CNBB and the Brazilian government joined forces to launch the *Movimento de Educação de Base* (MEB)—the Basic Education Movement. Brasília would provide funding for a series of radio schools to teach literacy. The radio schools were a reasonably efficient method to bring literacy training to the interior communities in the region. Lessons over the radio reached many more people than could be impacted by individual or group meetings.

The MEB cadres, or instructors, were often affiliated with AP or were certainly sympathetic to its interpretation of Brazilian reality. Many were university students who were associated with JUC in the past. It quickly became clear that the MEB was being highly influenced by the cadres' adoption of the general approach of *conscientização.* To further the mass literacy effort, MEB prepared a primer in 1963 called *Viver é Lutar* ("To Live Means to Struggle").

It quickly became clear to some in the Church hierarchy and to the conservative political right that the primer called for class warfare.

There had been a long-standing fear that efforts to introduce literacy would lead to social activism by the peasantry in the northeast. A new generation of younger political leaders committed to social justice and to a reasonable role for the marginal poor began to lobby for greater political representation for the poor. They argued that electoral politics were manipulated by the elites. The phrase "consciousness raising" became a rallying cry for the new activists. Literacy would allow the poor to make better political choices at election time, freeing them from the tradition of large landowners and political bosses buying their vote with simple handouts such as shoes or medicine.

A final area of "consciousness raising" in the late JK period and that of his short lived successor, Jânio Quadros, was the rural trade union movement. *Ligas Camponesas*—peasant leagues—had begun to spontaneously appear in the region in the late 1950s. Other rural-based organizations emerged but with little influence over policy. The Catholic Church had begun to organize rural unions at about the same period. But the Catholic radicals viewed rural syndicalism as an ideal vehicle for developing class consciousness or *conscientização*. With the passage of a Rural Labor Statute in March 1963, a race began by political groups across the spectrum to organize a" sindicato." The law stipulated that only one *sindicato* was allowed for each category of workers in a town. Once recognized by the Ministry of Labor, no other union organizing would be allowed by rival groups. Quickly, the government, the Catholic Church, radical nationalists, communists, and other organizers invaded the countryside in hopes of becoming the one recognized union—with obvious future electoral benefits.

What began as an analytical historical process in the 1950s with *ideal histórico* had morphed into a full-blown assault on the traditional institutions of Brazil. There is no doubt that the rise of Catholic radicalism added to the rapid polarization of the country in the late 1950s and early 1960s. The MEB, JUC, and rural unions were all seen by the elites as direct threats to their traditional dominance in the countryside. It became clear to the elites the process would need to be stopped—at any price.

Was the presidency of Jânio Quadros (1961) doomed to fail?

The last year of JK's presidency was far less successful than the bulk of his time in the presidential palace. Inflation and economic distress were widespread. In addition to the beginnings of Catholic radicalism, discussed previously, broader national questions were raised. Should illiterates be given the right to vote? Politics remained highly "clientelistic" and personalistic. Why did rural oligarchs continue to exercise undue weight in the Congress and at the state level in the north, west, and northeast? These concerns became highly salient in the politics of the early 1960s. The first sign of great "stress" in the system was the 1960 national election.

JK could not run again (but he was eligible to do so after the next presidential term of office). The PSD-PTB had no logical candidate to succeed JK; they turned with resignation to Marshal Henrique Lott, the "decision maker" in 1955. For the first time since 1946 the marginal UDN saw an opportunity to defeat the Getúlistas. Along with the small Christian Democratic Party (PDC), they tapped Jânio Quadros from São Paulo as their unity candidate. Quadros was charismatic and, in his own way, charming. He posed as a centrist and appeared to be whatever most of the voters wanted to believe he was. In the national election of October 1960, Quadros received 48 percent of the vote, against 28 percent for Lott, and 23 percent for Adhemar de Barros. The electorate was now 11.7 million strong. The new Vice President was Jango Goulart—running separately for the office. Immediately red flags went up on the right of the political spectrum.

Quadros quickly launched a new anti-inflation program; the cruzeiro was devalued effectively by 100 percent. While the Kubitschek years did represent a period of economic development, it also "broke the bank." Money was printed without concern for its impact on the overall economy. Kubitschek's policies to achieve his goals, especially the building of Brasília, were viewed as reckless by Quadros. Quadros was determined to overcome the prolifigacy of the JK "fifty years in five." Credit was squeezed, wages frozen, and import subsidies were slashed. He also personally supervised the efforts to reduce corruption and increase government efficiency. All of these measures were necessary to restore the health of the economy, but highly unfavorable to many groups in society. But the "medicine" worked—the United States and the IMF supported the program and new financing was secured; old debt was consolidated and extended. As the program appeared to be a success, Quadros began to have second thoughts. And many of the prominent anti-Getúlistas began to suspect that Quadros was attempting to be a more independent chief executive than they had hoped for. The UDN (conservative National Democratic Union party) leadership, especially Carlos Lacerda, now Governor of Guanabara state (today Rio de Janeiro), once again led the attack. Lacerda and his supporters were particularly concerned over what they saw as Quadros's move to the left on foreign policy. Personality differences also entered the debate. Totally without warning, Quadros submitted his resignation on April 25, 1961; it was immediately accepted by the Congress. Had he miscalculated? Did he hope for an outpouring of popular support? Frustrated with the frustrating ways of Brasília? We will never know.

Was Brazil about to see a repetition of the 1950s? Vice President Jango Goulart was the constitutional successor. But in the highly polarized political system, the anti-Getúlistas and some of the military high command immediately began a campaign to deny the presidency to Jango, who was on a visit to Communist China.

Could João Goulart have avoided the military coup of March 1964?

Whatever his motivation, the Quadros resignation once again divided the country. Brasília was stunned. The President of the Chamber was hurriedly sworn in as provisional president. It was clear that the military leadership would be decisive in determining the outcome of the crisis. The strategy of the military ministers was to have Jango declared ineligible by the Congress, given his absence from the country, and proceed to new elections in sixty days. Congress refused, although they appeared to be open to the creation of a parliamentary system, reducing the powers of the presidency. The political system stalemated. Suddenly, the commanding general in Jango's home state of RGS endorsed his accession to the presidency. The high command had fractured. The commander's position was supported by Leonel Brizola, the Governor of RGS (state of Rio Grande do Sul) and Jango's brother-in-law. Brizola was a rising star of the radical nationalist wing of the PTB (Brazilian Workers Party). As Jango's return appeared inevitable, civil society appeared to support the "legal" solution—follow the constitution. Jango, on his way back to Brazil, agreed to the installation of a Parliamentary system. He was sworn in on September 7, 1961.

Jango arrived in the presidential office with some advantages. He was the leader of the fastest growing party in the country, the PTB. While associated with Vargas, he was a relatively new face in national politics. As a compromise with the conservative military leaders and their associates in the legislature, a parliamentary system was installed; it lasted from September 1961 to January 1963. During that period, Jango tried to convince the doubters that he was a centrist but sympathetic to the social concerns of the radicals. He traveled to Washington, DC to meet with President John F. Kennedy and received a promise of $131 million in aid for supporting the efforts of SUDENE in the northeast. Created in the late 1950s,

The Superintendency for the Development of the Northeast (SUDENE) was an effort by the government to neutralize anti-reform forces in the region and to focus on a new strategy that would attempt to overcome many of the bottlenecks that, historically, had kept the region in a state of underdevelopment. Corruption of public funds, nepotism, and poor long-term planning were among the most important issues to be addressed. As a result, the US government would open one of the largest USAID missions in the world in the city of Recife, in the northeast state of Pernambuco.

Whatever his motivation, Jango began to support the idea of "basic reforms" to modernize Brazil. Very much reflecting the mood of the radicals, he called for land reform in a speech on May Day 1962, long anathema to the rural establishment that still retained considerable political influence. Politics in Brasília became highly unpredictable. Five prime ministers came and went during the parliamentary period. There began to be a feeling among political leaders that the system was not working; the presidential system had to be restored. As always, the military high command, if united, would have the last word. Jango had cultivated the armed forces with strategic promotions and appointments. The feeling in the presidential palace was that momentum favored a plebiscite. Elections for Congress and eleven governors in October confirmed the strength of the political center. The plebiscite was successfully held on January 6, 1963 to restore full presidential powers. The question on many minds was whether Jango was competent to exercise those powers democratically and transparently.

In historical perspective, the Goulart presidency was probably over as it started. The anti-Getúlistas were now out in full force. The radical nationalists were far in front of the president in demanding basic reforms; often vaguely, the president spoke frequently about land reform, opening the education system to the poor, and funding much needed medical facilities in the interior of the country, among other goals The industrial community in São Paulo began to organize in opposition to the government. Leonel Brizola, the president's brash brother-in-law, had been elected to Congress in October 1962 from Rio de Janeiro. He now became de facto leader of the radical left. The once dormant northeast was awakening and to the anti-Getúlistas it was tantamount to subversion. SUDENE, the Peasant Leagues, and the literacy program were all viewed by the conservative forces in the region as challenges to their centuries-old domination of all economic and political activities. The United States, as part of the Alliance for Progress in 1961, provided significant resources to support the developmental efforts of SUDENE to reduce the influence of those forces. In the context of the Cold War, the United States was concerned that the socioeconomic conditions in the northeast could be a justification for anti-American activity. After the victory of Fidel Castro in January 1959 in Cuba, Latin America appeared to be susceptible to Cuban influence, from the viewpoint of the United States.

For the first five months of his presidential term, Jango appeared committed to centrist reforms. He turned to one of the impressive new moderate reformist leaders, Celso Furtado, Superintendent of SUDENE, to develop a Three-Year Development Plan to control inflation and to reorganize the economy. Furtado was supported by San Tiago Dantas, the new Finance Minister, and an older representative of the moderate left. But neither individual had strong political support in the Congress. The plan collapsed in the summer of 1963. Jango agreed to salary raises for the military and the civil service that in fact destroyed the major objective of the plan—stop inflation. It became clear to an increasing number of analysts that the regime was beginning to move towards extreme polarization and possible collapse.

The remaining months of the Jango presidency saw increased contestation between the many "lefts" and the right in national and state politics. In September noncommissioned officers revolted in Brasília over their ineligibility to run for elective office. Insubordination was not acceptable in the military hierarchy. Politicians were unnerved by the ease with which the military men had basically seized control of Brasília. Jango requested a state of siege in October to allegedly control popular protests—but would he use it to punish his opponents? While supported by his military ministers who were responsible for law and order, Congress procrastinated and Jango withdrew the request.

The political situation deteriorated precipitately at the end of 1963. Secretly a group of high-ranking military officers began to consider a "defensive" strategy. The leader of the group was the new Army Chief of Staff, General Castelo Branco. Castelo Branco had been transferred from command of the Fourth Army, headquartered in Recife in the northeast, to a desk job in Rio. While stationed in Recife, he had witnessed the actions of the Peasant Leagues, the radicalization of the rural union movement, the MEB, and other challenges to the status quo. The economy deteriorated. The cabinet was subject to "musical chairs." The old debate about the appropriate role of foreign capital in the economy surfaced once again.

At the beginning of 1964, national attention began to focus on the 1965 presidential election. It was widely believed that the contest would force Brazilians to choose between candidates in the center of the political spectrum and those who favored basic reforms and more radical changes in Brazilian society such as uncompensated land reform.

The radical nationalists pushed their case for immediate basic reforms. They were able to convince the bewildered president that the only way to save his presidency was through determined action. On March, 13, 1964, the vacillating chief executive attended a huge rally in downtown Rio de Janeiro. To his dismay, his brother-in-law spoke and called for a Constituent Assembly to replace the elected Congress. The president signed two decrees in front of the crowd. The first nationalized all private oil refineries. The second called for the expropriation of "underutilized" properties located next to federal property. He indicated his next move would be to propose new legislation to give the vote to illiterates and enlisted servicemen, as well as a major tax reform that was assumed to be redistributive.

The military conspiracy was galvanized by the May rally. Castelo Branco circulated a memorandum to his staff that would justify military action, if needed, to preserve the constitutional order. On the weekend of March 27–29, there was a disciplinary crisis in the Navy. Jango hesitated and finally a full amnesty was ordered for the rebelling sailors. On March 19 a massive and spontaneous rally rally was held in São Paulo; others followed, clearly indicating the steadfast opposition of the middle class to the transpiring events.

In a speech on March 30 to a gathering of army sergeants, the president refused to criticize attacks on military discipline. The military interpreted the address as one more unnecessary affront to the armed forces. The decision was taken to remove the president in a bloodless coup d'état. Army units coordinated a movement to neutralize forces loyal to Goulart. Sensing that his presidency was about to end, the president left Brasília, stopped briefly in Rio de Janeiro, and then travelled to Porto Alegre, the capital of the state of Rio Grande do Sul. He met briefly with his brother-in-law, Leonel Brizola, who tried to convince the president to resist. Goulart refused and left Brazil for asylum in neighboring Uruguay.

The Jango Goulart government faced almost impossible expectations in 1961. The economic situation was rapidly deteriorating. Daily political life had become highly contentious and ideological. Class issues were front and center as everyone fought for shares of the national pie. Could Jango have survived if he had been a firm and articulate leader? Some speculate so; others argue that he was overwhelmed by the challenges he faced every day, and that the growing influence of the "evil" brother-in-law made him defensive and overwhelmed by events.

4

THE MILITARY IN POWER

THE FINAL INTERVENTION?

Did the first phase of the military government (1964–1967) offer any hope of a return to electoral democracy?

First and foremost, from the perspective of the military, Brazil's slide into a communist state had been stopped—and just in time. The task at hand, given the flight of Jango, was to restore constitutional order. The President of the Chamber of Deputies was sworn in as acting president for a maximum 30-day period. As speculation increased over the selection of the next chief executive, the political elites appeared unaware that the decision would be a military one without significant civilian input. The army was the institutional actor that would determine the course of Brazilian politics for the next twenty-one years.

In the preceding decade, the army had divided into two groups—although a small sector of independent officers remained. The first group was known as the *linha dura* or hardliners. They were insistent that it was the duty of the armed forces to assume and retain power in order to "cleanse" the political system and reorganize the national economy. They wanted little to do with elections, politicians, and specialized interest groups. The leader of the hardliners was General Artur da Costa e Silva, the new War Minister. He chose like-minded military officers from the Navy and Air Force to constitute a Supreme Revolutionary Command. After a brief dueling period with the Congress, the military ministers issued an Institutional Act on April 9 that dramatically expanded the powers of the presidency. That individual had total control over public spending; the authority to declare a state of siege; and the power to cancel for ten years the political rights of any citizen, and to cancel the mandate of any elected officials.

The next step was the selection of the president. The consensus candidate was General Castelo Branco. He was the natural leader of the second group in the army, the so-called "Sorbonne Group," closely associated with the Brazilian Higher War College. That institution had been modeled on the US National War College and became an influential center for debate about the country's future among civilians and military officers. Castelo Branco had served in the Brazilian Expeditionary Force in World War II and had spent time at the French Superior War College and at the US general command course at Fort Leavenworth. The Sorbonne group supported a free-enterprise economic system, a strong anticommunist foreign policy, and the modernization of Brazilian institutions to prepare the country for the restoration of democracy in the future. The vice-presidency went to a senior PSD politician from Minas Gerais and the cabinet was filled with senior members of the UDN and prominent anti-Getúlistas. The two key positions of Finance Minister and Planning and Economic Coordination were given to prominent monetarist and conservative political economists with the task of reorganizing the economy. Both appointees agreed that there was a serious fiscal imbalance in the national accounts. The government would need to reduce the public sector deficit, contract private credit, and stabilize wage rates. They also wanted an independent or autonomous Central Bank to preclude political pressures to print money. Huge deficits in state-owned enterprises had to be drastically reduced. To do so meant increasing the price of services, highly unpopular with the public. The government cracked down on tax enforcement, a long-standing problem in Brazil.

The economic challenge

As noted by Werner Baer, economic stabilization was the priority:

> The new military regime concluded that the path to economic recovery lay in control of inflation, elimination of accumulated price distortions, modernization of capital markets, creation of a system of incentives to direct investments into sectors deemed essential by the government, attraction of foreign investments to expand the country's productive capacity, and expansion of public investments in infrastructure projects and heavy industries.[1]

Government spending was cut, tax collection increased, wages were controlled, and access to credit curtailed. As a result, the government budget deficit declined. A 1965 capital market law provided a framework for strengthening the stock market. For the new government, foreign trade policy was key to an expansion of the economy and the diversification of exports. The economic team issued a 240-page Economic Action Program, 1964–1966 that provided the broad outlines of the recovery strategy for the Castelo Branco government. Debt renegotiation became imperative and was relatively successful. Attracting foreign capital was critical, and at the end of 1964 and 1965, financial support was provided by USAID, the World Bank, and the IMF. The country's creditworthiness had been restored—finally.

The political challenge

Critical to the new government was the dismantling of the radical nationalist network that, from the military viewpoint, had almost taken over the country. Thousands of those believed to be subversives were detained across the country. JUC and MEB were prominent victims. A wide range of subversive organizations were closed or driven underground. Labor organizers, rural and urban, were key targets, as were military officers and civil servants suspected of Getúlista sympathies. Many of those arrested were tortured. Key figures to lose their political rights for ten years included former presidents, governors, senators, and congressmen as well as diplomats, intellectuals, and journalists.

Within civil society, most groups supported the coup, including the Bar Association, the Roman Catholic Church, much of the media and, to be expected, the administration of President Lyndon Johnson and the American embassy in Rio de Janeiro, led by Ambassador Lincoln Gordon. While there was increasing dissent in the media over the reports of torture, the regime felt sufficiently confident to establish a political agenda. Although reluctant, Castelo Branco agreed to a Constitutional Amendment, extending his term of office to March 1967 and postponing the next presidential election to November 1966.

The regime also began an internal debate about the electoral process—to proceed or not? Local elections in São Paulo in March 1965 saw a candidate backed by Jânio Quadros as the winner. The hard-liners were not happy. The next set of elections was scheduled for governors in October 1965 and they were shaping up as a dual between the UDN, the principal backer of the government, and the PSD, the Getúlista political machine. The UDN lost in Guanabara (Rio de Janeiro) and Minas Gerais. While pro-government candidates won in the other nine state elections, the victory in two important states by candidates viewed as in opposition to the regime created a crisis. Unable to find a compromise between the hard-liners and the constitutionalists, Castelo Branco was forced to issue a Second Institutional Act on October 27 abolishing all political parties and making all future elections of president, vice president, and governor indirect. The Act also reconfirmed the president's powers to revoke an individual's political rights for ten years. It also "packed" the Supreme Court.

New party rules were announced and two political parties emerged. The government party, ARENA (National Renovation Alliance), and the small opposition, the MDB (Brazilian Democratic Movement), represented the new face of party politics in Brazil. By 1966, opposition was also centered increasingly in the Catholic Church, students, and a small group of subversives. In this context, the 1966 presidential succession became a matter of urgency. The Castelo Branco group was opposed to hardliner Costa e Silva but he had garnered widespread support across the army. In May 1966 ARENA endorsed the candidacy of the War Minister. The vice president was another seasoned politician from Minas Gerais. The MDB boycotted the election in Congress; Costa e Silva carried the vote on October 3. Federal and state legislative elections followed in November and the government party was triumphant.

The final item of business for the now-lame-duck Castelo Branco government was the drafting of a new constitution. The document strengthened the hand of the president and the federal government in all economic and political spheres. It was approved by Congress on January 24, 1967. The first phase of the 1964 "Revolution" was ending. Castelo Branco did his best to protect the overall goal of returning Brazil to democracy—at some point in the future. But the fury of the hardliners, the difficult economic impact of the stabilization program, and the fecklessness of the political class, especially in Congress, made his task overwhelming. Trying to pull Brazil back from the brink in 1964 was a formidable challenge. Castelo Branco did the best he could by preserving the shell of democracy: elections, if indirect; a temporary slow-down in torture and repression that would still return later in the regime; and supporting his economic team in implementing a difficult adjustment program. But the successful adjustment would only motivate the hardliners in the next decade to deepen "their" revolution that focused on further repression, greater authoritarianism, and less room for dissent.

Did the economic "miracle" of the late 1960s/early 1970s prolong the military regime?

Costa e Silva was inaugurated on March 15, 1967. As one commentator noted,

> The new president fit the stereotype of the Latin American military officer. He was jovial, more at home at the horse races than studying tomes on military strategy. The apparent contrast with the austere, intellectual Castelo Branco could hardly have been greater, but that contrast in images was not entirely accurate.[2]

Costa e Silva had served in the Brazilian embassy in Buenos Aires and he had spent six months at Fort Knox. He had also commanded the Fourth Army in Recife in 1961–1962 as Catholic radicalism was at its apogee in the northeast. The new president decided on a major turnover in personnel. There were no holdovers from the Castelo Branco camp. A number of military officers were appointed to the cabinet and other key posts. A critical choice was that of a young economist from São Paulo, Antônio Delfim Neto, as the new Finance Minister. The new government was basically composed of hardliners with few of the affinities for the United States that the Castelo Branco team had.

The economy

Delfim and his team inherited an economy well on the way to recovery—even if it was not widely recognized. Contrary to Campos and the Castelo Branco group, he believed that the economy needed a new look. The most important cost was credit which had been tightened from 1964–1967. Delfim and his "boys" decided to take a new direction—stimulate demand by easing credit. It would turn out to be a brilliant, if dangerous, decision. What could have been a challenge to the new formula, the labor unions, proved to be controllable. The government retained the power to set the minimum wage even though it was clear working-class incomes were actually declining. Control of the labor unions was easily dealt with through the Ministry of Labor and protests.

Delfim's pragmatism worked. Foreign direct investment flowed. International agencies continued to supply credit. This allowed the government to finance current account deficits. Tax policy was revised to reduce the share of federal revenues that was transferred to the state and municipal governments, freeing up resources for federal programs. Growth picked up and Brazil was about to enter the period of the "miracle"—GDP growth was 11 percent and would continue in that range until the first oil price shock in 1973–1974. There was strong growth in the industrial and agricultural sectors. Exports expanded impressively—especially non-coffee exports.

Politics

Having made the decision to allow political institutions to function (albeit in truncated form) in contrast to the policies of the other "bureaucratic-authoritarian" regimes, the powerful civilian bureaucracies supported by the armed forces that were emerging in Latin America, the regime had to deal with the political process. A principal opponent was the journalist Carlos Lacerda. He had organized a "Broad Front" of opposition leaders shortly after the coup. He announced his candidacy for the 1971 presidential election. Lacerda gained the support of Jango Goulart for the Broad Front, but not that of his brother-in-law. Kubitschek had endorsed the Front earlier. It called for a return to democracy and economic liberalism. Viewed as a political threat to the government, within a short time Lacerda was banned from politics.

Another bone of contention became student politics. Protests, often violent, began in 1968. In March a student leader was killed by the police and a massive march ended in a memorial mass at the Candelaria Cathedral in downtown Rio de Janeiro. Further incidents of violence continued. Marches were banned by the government amid continuing debate over the need for a basic reform of the higher education system, which was old fashioned and not suited to a Brazil in the middle of the 20th century. This was a critical policy issue for the now-famous middle class. University education was viewed as critical for social mobility and economic success.

A third opposition force emerged in April 1968 with the first industrial strike since 1964. The decline in real wages was the driver behind the demonstrations. Increasingly, industrial workers were ignoring and bypassing government-appointed labor leaders and interacting directly with their employers. The government seemed at a loss. The metalworkers were the most militant of the industrial workers—Luiz Inácio "Lula" da Silva, a future president, would begin his political career as part of the workers' demonstrations.

Slowly, a "progressive" wing of the Catholic Church emerged. The CNBB issued a working paper in July 1968 condemning the government's national security doctrine. The leader in this movement was Dom Hélder Pessoa Câmara, now the Archbishop of Recife in the northeast. The progressives highlighted social injustice, torture, and the worsening economic situation of the working class.

The hardliners began to fear that these trends could lead to massive rejection of the revolutionary model. Their concern was exacerbated by worldwide student demonstrations in 1968. Students were an important part of the growing opposition in the United States to the war in Vietnam. At home, a little known congressman, Márcio Moreira Alves, delivered a series of speeches calling for Brazilians to keep their children at home and away from the September 7 Independence Day ceremonies. He also urged Brazilian women to withhold their favors from military men until the regime cancelled torture and police brutality.

To no one's surprise, the hardliners were livid. They demanded that the president "do something." What they wanted was the lifting of political immunity for those members of Congress they saw as "subversive." After furious debate, the Congress defeated the motion of the government on December 12, 1968. To the surprise of the government, ninety-four members of ARENA voted with the majority.

The hardliners were even more apoplectic after the vote and pressured the government to do something even more stringent. The president convened the National Security Council on December 13; that night a new Institutional Act was issued that closed Congress indefinitely. The Act opened a long process of repression. Journalists were arrested; many politicians lost their political rights; state legislatures were suspended; all state military and police forces were put under the authority of the War Minister; university professors were involuntarily retired. On a "positive" note, from the perspective of the regime, a new curriculum was launched that promoted patriotism at every level of education.

In response to the growing civil unrest, a new, harsher constitution was drafted in 1969. Another Institutional Act, the Fifth, was issued—it had no expiration date and it gave the executive the right to suspend habeas corpus for as long as the authorities wished to do so. The hardliners were triumphant. It appeared as though there were no safeguards against their relentless campaigning for harsher authoritarian measures.

A guerrilla threat

In the midst of both rapid economic growth and political discontent, a major threat to the regime emerged that gave the hardliners even greater influence in setting the policy agenda. Young militants on the radical left—many with affiliation with JUC, AP, and MEB—among others, decided to challenge the regime with bombings, bank robberies, and kidnappings. This was not a plan of the traditional Communist Party (PCB), a cautious nonviolent organization. Indeed, frustrated members of the PCB defected to the armed guerrilla movement and served in leadership positions. This was not a unified movement. It contained younger military officers, some of whom had been dismissed in 1964; middle-class students; and dissident union members.

The regime reacted with widespread imprisonment and torture. Two events brought the untenable situation to a crescendo. On August 29 the president suffered a stroke from which he would not recover. There was a crisis in the leadership of the regime. The military ministers assumed de facto power. They decided immediately that the civilian vice president would be overlooked and ignored. A weeks-long process of intra-military consultation resulted in the choice of Costa e Silva's close friend, General Emílio Garrastazu Médici; a ranking admiral was selected as vice president. Congress was recalled and rubber-stamped the military candidates. A new Institutional Act stated that the new presidential term would end on March 15, 1974. An amendment to the 1967 constitution basically created a new document that was issued on October 17, 1969. The 1969 amendment basically incorporated most of the policy initiatives set in motion since 1964. It also increased the authority of the central government over key decisions without the need to consult Congress.

In the midst of the uncertainty over the presidential succession, the urban guerrillas carried out an audacious operation: the kidnapping of the US ambassador on September 4. The kidnappers demanded that the government broadcast their revolutionary manifesto within forty-eight hours and that fifteen imprisoned guerrillas be released—their names were specified. A fierce debate took place within the high command. Finally, under strong pressure from the US government, the two demands were met. The liberated guerrillas left Brazil on September 7 for exile in Mexico. A further round of arrests took place and the grip of the hardliners over government policy was even greater. For many officers in the armed forces it was incomprehensible that the country did not understand the need for security and did not recognize the success of the regime in producing historic rates of economic growth. The "miracle" was obvious, to the military. Why not to the general public? Determined to continue with its "revolutionary" mandate, the armed forces were able to destroy the guerrilla movement within a few years.

Torture was an issue of growing concern during the Médici government. Human rights groups in the United States openly criticized the regime. The Pope denounced torture and alluded to the case of Brazil. Hearings were held in the US Senate. But the government chose to wait patiently for the furor to dissipate. It did, slowly, and it was helped with the election of President Richard Nixon in 1968. The United States invited President Médici to Washington, DC on a state visit in December 1971 and he was fêted at the White House. Members of the Nixon administration visited Brazil and returned with praise for the economic "miracle." It was also clear that the strong anticommunist posture of the Brazilian regime was deeply supported by the White House.

Was the Médici government the apex of the 1964 "revolution?"

Reeling from the guerrilla threat and the kidnapping of the American ambassador, the Médici government used repression and censorship to maintain order. An important part of the success of the regime was increasing wealth and employment opportunities for middle-class citizens, although the poor, rural, and urban saw little benefit from what was now termed "Grandeza" (Greatness)—Brazil was putting behind centuries of backwardness and moving to new heights of development and greater global recognition of its achievements (even though the 1970 Census confirmed that the country's distribution of income had grown more unequal). A technocratic government brought order and discipline to the economy; the armed forces provided the "cover" for the system to function without dissent. The regime organized a highly visible public relations campaign—both internal and external—to highlight the success of the Revolution.

Popular sentiment was assuaged by Brazil winning the World Cup in the soccer tournament in Mexico in 1970; having won three times, Brazil was able to retire the Trophy. Slowly the middle class felt comfortable with the regime and its successes, since they were major beneficiaries. The political opposition appeared to be in permanent limbo. The regime undertook a National Integration Program (PIN) that focused on the drought-stricken northeast. The answer to the historical problem of the region was the decision to construct a Transamazon Highway that would open the Amazon valley to immigrants from the poor northeast. Other public works projects—the expansion of the national highway system—dominated the closing years of the "Grandeza" period in Brazilian history.

The closing year of the administration saw a renewed debate over the presidential succession. Concerned with a slow reemergence of the legal opposition, especially at the state level, the government decided to postpone direct election for governors, scheduled for 1974, until 1978. Unnoticed by the hardliners, the *castelistas* in the Armed Forces were plotting a return to power. They gained the support of the army minister, Orlando Geisel, when they selected his brother, Ernesto, as their candidate. Geisel was announced as the ARENA candidate in June 1973. He was duly elected by an electoral college in January 1974.

With hindsight, the "recapturing" of the Planalto (presidential palace) in Brasília by the *castelistas* signaled the end of the most repressive years of the 1964 Revolution. The way forward would not be preordained, but the final decade of the 1964 Revolution was underway. The economic "miracle" and the hype over *grandeza,* plus the ruthless repression of all dissent, gave the impression that the hardliners would rule forever. That was not to be true and the final decade of the 1964 Revolution would be a difficult and often unpredictable journey.

Could the Geisel administration have acted more expeditiously to end the repressive regime?

It was clear, within military ranks at least, that the Geisel administration had to follow a careful path to political liberalization—a long-time *castelista* goal. The first challenge was to maintain the unity of the armed forces, the sine qua non of exercising political power. The government would need to undertake the delicate task of moving the military out of politics—and out of the sordid record of repression and torture. There was also concern over the expanding power of the SNI (National Intelligence Service), which was increasingly seen as the enforcer of the policies favored by the most conservative actors in the government.

SNI operatives were also seen as crowding out the professional officer corps. It was also important for the Geisel government to be seen as vigilant on pursuing subversive elements in Brazilian society. While the guerrilla movement was a thing of the past, the security forces were always able to fabricate new enemies of the state.

As the debate about political liberalization began in 1974, two realities were front and center. The first was the need to address the growing income inequality. While the miracle years had rewarded the middle and upper-middle sectors of society, they had not done so for the disadvantaged. And the issue was whether the advantaged segment of the population—about twenty-two million—was a sufficiently large and dynamic market to sustain a high rate of economic growth. Another way of looking at the question was whether or not Brazil was developing a dual society—one Brazil growing wealthier while the other stagnated.

The second and critical issue was economic growth. Unfortunately, the Geisel administration entered office in the context of the first oil shock of November 1973 that quadrupled the price of imported petroleum. Brazil at the time imported about 80 percent of its petroleum; suddenly the import bill skyrocketed. The government had two choices: reduce growth to reduce the annual cost of importing oil or choose to continue with high rates of growth that would mean acquiring substantial amounts of foreign debt. The latter option was the one chosen. At the time, given the political need for continued growth, and the fact of low international interest rates, it was reasonable to think it was the right decision.

In the context of *distensão* (liberalization), the Geisel economic team went to work. They produced a Second National Development Plan (1975–1979) that deepened import substitution industrialization in areas such as steel, aluminum, fertilizers, and petrochemicals. The Plan also gave priority to infrastructure with large investments in transportation, communication, and alcohol production. All of these measures aimed at reducing the import bill. But it soon became clear that increasing foreign debt would be needed to sustain the plan.

As it struggled with the new development challenges, the Geisel government was confronted with a surge in electoral strength of the opposition MDB party. As talk of liberalization or decompression—a slow but deliberate process to begin to expand democratic space—continued, there was a sudden surge of support for the opposition. Brazilians began to believe that the Geisel government was sincere in its signaling for more openness. The congressional elections in November produced a landslide for the opposition. The MDB almost doubled its representation in the Chamber of Deputies. The MDB won almost five million more votes than ARENA in the Senate races. The MDB also did well in the race for state legislatures in some of the largest states. With the MDB controlling more than one-third of the votes in Congress, the government had lost the two-thirds majority it needed to amend the constitution. And the election results demonstrated how weak ARENA had become through its subservient support for the most repressive period of the Revolution.

The government was under ongoing pressure from the Catholic Church and the Brazilian Bar Association over continued cases of torture. Two cases of widely publicized cases of death by torture in São Paulo in 1975 and 1976 forced President Geisel to dismiss the commanding General of the army in the state. He did so without consulting the high command, a decision without precedent. For the first time, the hardliners began to understand that the government was serious about respecting civil liberties, unlike its predecessors.

Throughout his time in office, Geisel had to walk a fine line between the still influential hardliners and the growing pressure from the Church, the lawyers, the press, and now the MDB. To retain military support the government, in April 1977, closed the Congress and announced a series of constitutional changes, clearly aimed at limiting the future success of the MDB and hoping to restore some of its lost luster to the ARENA. In a risky decision in October 1977, the president summarily fired the Army Minister, a leader of the hardliners. The army accepted the decision to the relief of the Planalto—the presidential palace in Brasília.

The next challenge for the government was the presidential succession of 1978. Geisel was determined to select a candidate who would continue the *castelista* reforms, modest as they were, up to that time. General João Baptista Figueiredo, the SNI director, was announced as the ARENA candidate in April 1978. He was elected by the ARENA-dominated electoral college in October. In a signal of further decompression, the government allowed 120 political exiles to return to Brazil—Leonel Brizola and Luís Carlos Prestes were excluded.

The final political development of the Geisel administration was the emergence of organized labor, long dormant. The rapid process of industrialization had created a much larger work force in and around São Paulo—younger, healthier, and with far less respect for the straitjacketed regulations of the Ministry of Labor. Strikes, walkouts, and sit-ins suddenly became a daily occurrence. The most prominent leader of the new generation was "Lula" (Luiz Inácio da Silva), president of the Metalworkers Union, located in the important industrial suburb of São Bernardo. A major cause for the new union members was the deliberate decision of the government to fail to adjust fully for inflation when new minimum wage rates were set. The new unionists would become a potent force in national politics in the years ahead.

In retrospect, the Geisel government accomplished a great deal. *Habeas corpus* was restored; press censorship was lifted; political refugees were allowed to return; Institutional Act 5, the most egregious of the Acts issued since 1964, was canceled. And perhaps most important, he had tamed the hardliners. They had not disappeared but they had come to grudgingly respect the authority of the president even if they disagreed with specific decisions.

Did the Figueiredo government help or hinder the final years of the decompression?

When President Figueiredo entered office he was seen as a "bridge" between the Médici and Geisel administrations. He had served in both in increasingly senior positions. He was viewed as an amiable, social individual, in sharp contrast with his dour Protestant predecessor. His skills were quickly put to the test. Simmering discontent among the new unionists broke out in March 1979 when the metalworkers—critical to the booming automobile industry in São Paulo—walked off the job. Wage issues were at the top of their list of demands but they also wanted recognition of independent union spokesmen who were not linked to the government. While not achieving all of their demands, they had established their importance both in the industrial sector and in national politics. They had forced their employers to negotiate directly with the unions without government mediation. They had rallied support from the Church and many middle-class professionals. The metalworkers also served as an inspiration for other workers to follow their lead in organizing strikes and other disruptive events.

On the economic front, the news was very troubling. The second oil shock in 1979 further challenged the priorities of the regime. The new Planning Minister wanted to slow growth and stabilize the situation. After eleven years of impressive growth, no one was in the mood for retrenchment. Under increasing pressure to reverse course, the Planning Minister resigned and Antônio Delfim Netto, who was the architect of the "miracle," was reappointed. Rapid growth was again the raison d'etre of the government. Delfim issued a Third Development Plan, 1980–1986 but it virtually ignored the Achilles' heel of the economy: growing inflation combined with a scarcity of foreign exchange. His answer was a maxi-devaluation in December 1979; the situation would not improve for the rest of the Figueiredo term in office. The economy was severely impacted by the default of the Mexican government in August 1982. International bankers became increasingly wary about new loans for countries like Brazil. Delfim had no choice but to open negotiations with the IMF in late 1982, once again opening the debate about international capitalist control of the Brazilian economy. The economy would lurch from one emergency measure to another until the transition in 1985.

On the political front, the issue of amnesty was front and center. An amnesty bill was approved by Congress in August 1979—all of the old "subversives" were included. A second challenge was the political party system. Clearly, the government party, ARENA, had lost its legitimacy. General Golbery do Couto e Silva, one of the architects of the decompression process, supported a return to a multiparty system. It was approved by Congress in November 1979. ARENA regrouped as the Democratic Social Party (PSD) and the MDB added "P" (Party) and moved ahead. A number of smaller parties emerged as well. The most interesting new organization was the Workers Party (PT) of Lula, created in October 1979. The PT would serve as a constant opposition to any government in power until it was finally elected in 2002.

The 1980–1981 period saw the reaction of the hardliners to the decompression process. A series of bombings shocked the country. The most serious took place in Rio de Janeiro in

April 1981. General Golbery do Couta e Silva, the president's chief political advisor, called for a full investigation. Any talk of greater political freedom was not acceptable. Golbery, the strongest advocate of greater political freedom, decided he could no longer stem the influence of the conservative military officers and bureaucrats. The president refused to do so; Golbery resigned; the hardliners had made their point.

The November 1982 state elections were the last prior to the presidential election in 1985. They were open and transparent. The opposition carried most of the major states. The government did reasonably well in Congressional elections but it lost its absolute majority in the lower house. As 1983 opened, the presidential succession became the principal topic of conversation. President Figueiredo has suffered a heart attack in 1981 and had bypass surgery in 1983. His ill health introduced a note of uncertainty into the political equation. With the presidential election still indirect, would the president have the strength—and temperament—to guide the process?

Suddenly, a national campaign for direct presidential elections erupted nationwide. The campaign galvanized Brazilian society. Politicians, soccer stars, singers, the media, and the general public rallied in most of the cities across the country. Congress considered a constitutional amendment in April 1983 but it lost by a small margin. The opposition was determined to avoid confrontation and to use peaceful means to influence the outcome of the indirect vote in the Electoral College in January 1985. The PDS nominated Paulo Maluf as their presidential candidate, a long time politician from São Paulo, who was often at the center of alleged corruption scandals. An important wing of the PDS left the party to organize a Liberal Front. The PMDB turned to a veteran political leader from Minas Gerais, Tancredo Neves. The Liberal Front joined the PMDB campaign, organizing a Democratic Alliance, and named the vice president, former PDS leader José Sarney. On January 15, 1985 the Electoral College elected the candidates of the Democratic Alliance. The president had decided to remain neutral; the military accepted the results as long as the legalities were observed. The election took place in the context of an improving economy. The severe recession of 1981–1983 was apparently over, providing a breathing space for the new government.

With hindsight, the last military government facilitated the transition. It allowed dissidents to return to active politics with the amnesty. It accepted the results of the November 1982 elections. It allowed the Electoral College to function and it had the good grace to accept defeat. It could have been different if the armed forces had decided that they could not yet accept a civilian government, but they did not.

Mercosur—the Common Market of the South—Was it part of the transition from military rule and could it have succeeded?

The 20th century saw a number of initiatives to pursue regional economic integration in Latin America. In 1960, member states created the Latin American Free Trade Association (LAFTA) and the Latin American Integration Association (LAIA) in 1980. Both efforts were strongly supported by The United Nations Economic Commission for Latin America and the Caribbean (ECLAC, based in Santiago, Chile). ECLAC also oversaw the establishment of the Central American Common Market, also in 1960, and the Andean Group in 1969. As part of this tradition of seeking greater integration regional integration, Argentina and Brazil in 1985 signed the Declaration of Iguazu that created a bilateral commission to promote the integration of their economies; by the next year the two neighbors had negotiated several commercial agreements.

In the specific cases of Argentina (1983) and Brazil (1985), both countries had just transitioned from a military dictatorship to a democratic system of government. Both countries hoped that economic integration would lessen the military nationalism that had characterized relations between the two republics earlier and to put to rest the centuries-old rivalry that often threatened civilian rule. The 1988 Treaty for Integration,

Cooperation, and Development committed Argentina and Brazil to work toward the establishment of a common market within ten years and invited other Latin American countries to join.

Mercosur was created in 1991 by the Treaty of Asunción which was signed by the heads of state of Argentina, Brazil, Paraguay, and Uruguay (the latter two nations had recently restored democratic governance). In 1994, the Ouro Preto Protocol established Mercosur's present organizational structure and gave it a legal personality under international law, allowing it to negotiate agreements with countries and other international organizations. On January 1, 1995, following several years of efforts to reduce internal tariffs, a free trade zone and customs union were formally established. Nevertheless, full harmonization eluded Mercosur; some internal goods were still subject to customs duties, and though members agreed to apply a common tariff on imports from nonmembers, disparities on such duties continued to exist. In 1996, the Joint Parliamentary Commission, consisting of parliamentarians from member countries, declared that all participating members must have functioning democratic institutions.

Mercosur signed a free-trade agreement with the Andean Community that went into effect on July 1, 2004. Several countries were later admitted to Mercosur as associate members and in 2006 the presidents of the four member countries approved full membership for Venezuela (strongly supported by Brazil), though its final ascent was blocked for years by the Congress of Paraguay, which argued the government in Caracas did not respect democracy.

In 2012, following the controversial impeachment of Paraguayan President Fernando Lugo, that country was suspended until 2013, the time of the next elections in Paraguay. At the same summit, leaders from the three active members agreed to grant Venezuela full membership, effective July 31, 2012. In another step toward deeper regional integration, the Union of South American Nations (UNASUR) had been created as a regional customs union in 2008 with hope of combining Mercosur and the Andean Community in the future.

From its early promise, a number of issues have hindered the fulfillment of the original goal of Mercosur. Economic and financial crises, at different times, have created uncertainty about the feasibility of deeper integration. There is no comprehensive dispute mechanism in the organization; all decisions must be taken by consensus by the presidents of the individual countries. Tariff disputes continue to obstruct full cooperation. The addition of Venezuela to Mercosur has raised a number of questions as to whether or not the organization has now become politicized. The Venezuelan government, following the political ideology of Hugo Chavez, it's now deceased leader, argues that Mercosur should fight for social justice and combat market capitalism.

Mercosur represents one moment in the region's desire for greater cooperation and integration. But after what appeared to be a successful takeoff, the organization has drifted and many believe that its best years are in the past. While its headquarters in Montevideo, Uruguay continues to function, there appears little of substance that results from its deliberations.

The Military and Artistic Expression in Brazil

One of the many anomalies of the Brazilian military dictatorship (1964–1985) was the burgeoning of a strong counterculture of writers and artists. It seemed to many that the greater the repression by the armed forces, the stronger the effort by Brazil's artistic community to express itself. This reflected the growing tensions in Brazilian society in the 1950s and early 1960s that we have discussed earlier in this book. With the beginnings of the breakdown of the 1946 Republic we saw the rise of peasant leagues, adult literacy programs, debates about consciousness raising, and other challenges to the conservative social and political order. With the overthrow of the government in March 1964, there was, at first, little effort to systemically repress artistic expression of the left. This changed dramatically in the late 1960s as guerrilla groups and student protests erupted across Brazil and a long period of repression began, only culminating with the decompression or opening in the late 1970s.

After 1968, many political rights were suspended and the regime, confronted with increased militancy, resorted to detention, torture, and murder to neutralize their opponents. Civil society reacted. Massive and peaceful demonstrations began to appear in which the Roman Catholic Church, trade unions, student organizations and, increasingly, liberal professionals marched together. As a result of the actions of the military regime, many left-of-center academics, professionals, journalists, and artists were forced into exile.

Among the many that remained in Brazil there were, of course, wide-ranging debates within the cultural community about the best way to demonstrate their opposition to the dictatorship but to retain their freedom to do so. As Claudio Calirman has written, writers and artists began to discuss

> How to reconcile the political agenda with artistic innovation in a country under censorship? Could artists be at once politically active on a local level and engaged in international artistic development? Could they find an alternative to conventional models of social activism, which almost always sacrificed aesthetic quality for ideological agenda?[3]

Many of the artists of that period chose to impose self-censorship. Fearing persecution, they sought to write and paint anonymously and they decided to abandon traditional forms of artistic expression and to try and shock Brazilian society into recognizing the new realities of daily life. But caution was critical. International events began to impinge on the degree of freedom that the artistic community could enjoy. The US government supported the military regime out of fear of communism in the region. Che Guevara, the Cuban revolutionary, was killed in Bolivia. John F. Kennedy, the US president, had been assassinated in 1963 and Martin Luther King, the leader of the civil rights movement, was murdered in 1968. The Soviet Union had invaded Czechoslovakia and hundreds of student demonstrators were killed in a bloody confrontation with the Mexican government.

The Brazilian artistic community was well aware of the externalities that existed. Their struggle was one of many in a rapidly changing global context. They could expect little if any support from the outside world. Their challenge, they believed, was to use their talents to challenge the dictatorship but with the realization that it was a struggle they might not win. The regime began to cancel art exhibits and to confiscate works of arts that were considered subversive. The media was heavily censored and told not to provide coverage of anti-regime art. Intimidation became a favored weapon of the regime.

The high point of the early period of artistic opposition took place in 1969. It was over the X São Paulo Biennial, the premier venue for artistic innovation and exposure for Brazilian artists to international trends. The first Biennial was held in 1951 and quickly became the point of contact for Brazilian artists with the colleagues from around the world. In preparation for the 1969 Biennial, international artists decided to boycott the show. France, long a cultural model for Brazil, refused to participate. Many other countries followed. The foreign press covered the controversial circumstances of the 1969 Biennial and the military regime was deeply offended and embarrassed.

The Biennial controversy took place as the military regime was deepening its control over the media and any form of protest. It was also the height of the economic boom in Brazil and national pride, particularly among conservative social circles and the armed forces, was aghast at the worldwide negative publicity. While the early 1970s saw little artistic innovation, the middle of the decade saw the beginnings of the relaxation of the security controls and the slow but certain reemergence of the Brazilian artistic community. Exiles began to return and new forms of expression were tolerated, if at times barely, by the most reactionary forces in the regime. But the turning point was real. The dark days of censorship and repression ended in the early 1980s. Brazilian art, theater, and music have thrived ever since.

5

FAILED TRANSITION?

The military regime was ending but what would come next for what was termed the "New Republic?" Tancredo Neves was viewed as a great unifier. As he prepared for his inauguration on March 15, 1985, a long-standing illness worsened and he fell ill on the eve of the ceremony. Following a short debate, José Sarney was sworn in as "Acting President," on the assumption that Neves would return shortly to assume office. But he died on April 27 in São Paulo. Sarney was now the constitutional chief executive. Sarney had never expected to become president. A genial man of the legislature, he had survived decades of political turmoil by knowing how to be cooperative with whoever held power. Sarney agreed that a Constituent Assembly needed to be convened to write a new document for a democratic Brazil. Sarney and the Congress, working together, restored direct presidential elections; illiterates were again given the right to vote; political parties that met minimal registration requirements were recognized; and direct elections for mayors were restored. November 15, 1985 was set as the first election. The old government party, the PDS, did poorly. The PMDB won nineteen of the twenty-five capitals but lost São Paulo, Rio de Janeiro, and Porto Alegre. Divisive populist figures reemerged such as Jânio Quadros as mayor of São Paulo and candidates supported by Leonel Brizola in Rio de Janeiro and RGS.

But the principal challenge, once again, was inflation. It had reached 150 percent in 1983, over 200 percent in 1984, and by February 1986 about 300 percent. The Sarney government came under increasing pressure to address the issue. The president's popularity was dropping each month; the media were urging emergency measures. Desperate, Sarney took the advice of his Finance Minister and, in a national TV address on February 28, 1986, announced a "heterodox" adjustment program. The aim was to destroy inflation once and for all. The "Cruzado Plan" (the name of the new currency) had the following prescriptions: a general price freeze; a wage freeze following an increase; and a wage escalation system that guaranteed an automatic wage increase whenever the consumer price index rose 20 percent from the previous adjustment. The early results were extraordinarily impressive. Inflation all but disappeared. But then it didn't. The easy fix worked—for a while. But the longer the freeze lasted, the more market distortions emerged. While economists agreed the price freeze should be temporary, there was no consensus on how long it should remain in place. Over the next few months, politics took over from economics. The price freeze was extremely popular with the public. But the political cost of lifting it became too much of a challenge for the presidential palace. And there were national elections scheduled for November and zero inflation was the government's "ticket" to victory in November. Attempts to circumvent the freeze emerged. The Cruzado Plan was a consumer-driven event. Sarney was reluctant to change anything since the Plan had been his road to success and the happy consumers were the voters in November.

The government reached the elections—barely. But the impression among the public was that all would be well. The PMDB won twenty-two of the twenty-three governorships in play and won absolute majorities in both houses of Congress. With victory at hand, the government announced Cruzado II. It took the "bloom off the rose"—prices increased dramatically for many consumer goods and services. Inflation returned, reaching 2000 percent in June 1987. The government had declared a unilateral moratorium on its debt the previous February. For all intents and purposes, the Sarney administration had declared bankruptcy—economic and political. During the remaining time of his presidency, there were a series of short-stop stabilization programs that did not work, revolving-door Finance Ministers, and a loss of confidence on the part of the country's creditors.

The president cultivated the military, which was in turn pleased to be at the center of power once again. A new Constitution was promulgated in 1988. Sarney's principal concern was having his term extended from four to five years; he succeeded in that regard, but the price of his success was often giving into congressional pressures for spending measures, further exacerbating inflation. While the new Constitution guaranteed Sarney five years in office, it was regressive in another way. It required that the federal government transfer 21.5 percent of the income tax and manufactured goods tax to the states and municipalities but "forgot" to transfer responsibility for programs such as education and housing as well. These obligations remained federal and created significant lack of equilibrium in the federal budget.

Eyes quickly turned to the next presidential election scheduled for October 15, 1989. Public opinion polls indicated that the PMDB would do very poorly, being blamed for the failure of the Cruzado Plan and the return of inflation. The country wanted something new. Unfortunately, it got what it wished for. Suddenly, a new face appeared—Fernando Collor de Mello—from the small, impoverished state of Alagoas in the northeast. He railed against the "maharajas" (unaccountable big spenders) in the government; he called for fiscal probity; and he offered a new generation of leaders, untainted by the military regime. His principal opponent was Lula, the PT leader, who was making the first of four runs for the presidency. The Lula of 1989 was a strident, union-oriented leftist in the eyes of the establishment. They opted for the lesser of two evils and backed Collor in the second round of voting; he won with 53 percent of the vote. The inauguration was held in March 1990, ending the Sarney era.

There is very little good to be said about the Sarney government. He did preside, more or less, over reestablishing democratic institutions. A new constitution was written. Respect for civil liberties was restored. But his utter failure to understand the potential—and then real—damage of the Cruzado Plan doomed the historical record of his administration. After the failure of the Plan, the country drifted, angry and sullen. Only the strong support of the military for his presidency, and the near total chaos in Congress, guaranteed that he would end his term peacefully and legally.

Was the Collor de Mello government doomed to fail?

With little support in Congress, the new president launched another heterodox shock program. The principal components were the freezing of 80 percent of all deposits in financial accounts for eighteen months; a new currency, the cruzeiro; a one-time tax on financial transactions; an initial price and wage freeze; an increase in the price of public services; liberalization of the exchange rate; and measures to reduce tax evasion. Little noticed was the unveiling of preliminary measures to begin a process of privatization. The immediate impact of the program was to sharply reduce the country's liquidity, which resulted in a pronounced drop in economic activity. Inflation did decline initially, but as price and wage controls were loosened, inflation returned.

Suddenly, in the middle of 1992, Pedro Collor, the president's disgruntled brother, revealed a system of corruption that had been instituted at the beginning of the administration. Faced with impeachment in September 1992, he resigned the presidency only hours before the Senate approved his conviction on grounds of official malfeasance (he later returned to the federal Senate from his home state). He was succeeded by his little-known vice president, Itamar Franco.

Collor did take a series of measures to liberalize the economy in his short time in office. He gave priority to privatizing state companies. He supported deregulation and reduced tariffs to open the economy to more competition. These initiatives were a promising start to a process that would "take off" in the succeeding decade. But his arrogance and inability to work with Congress, combined with his appointment of less than competent public servants who oversaw helter-skelter shock programs, doomed his presidency. The corruption issue—that had been the center of his campaign for the presidency—was the last straw for the Brazilian public.

Was Fernando Henrique Cardoso the right choice to defeat Brazilian inflation?

Collor de Mello was succeeded by his vice president, Itamar Franco. An erratic, if at times feisty, politician, he was very much of a stand-in until the next presidential election. Inflation remained the principal policy challenge under Itamar's watch. After three short-lived Ministers of Finance, he turned to his foreign minister, Fernando Henrique Cardoso.

Cardoso had been active in politics for some years. He was a well-known sociologist and writer. For his antiregime conduct under the military, he was exiled first to Chile and then to France. Returning to Brazil after the 1979 amnesty, he became active in the *Diretas Já* campaign in the early 1980s to restore direct presidential elections in 1985. Cardoso was also a founding member of the Brazilian Center for Analysis and Planning (CEBRAP), supported by the Ford Foundation. The Center brought together many of the liberal academics in São Paulo in the darkest days of the dictatorship. Cardoso ran for the federal Senate in 1978 and finished second in the race, winning 1.2 million votes. When the front runner became governor of the state of São Paulo in 1982, Cardoso automatically succeeded him in the federal Senate, taking his seat in March 1983. He established an impressive record in the Senate. When Itamar Franco succeeded Collor de Melo, he asked Cardoso to become foreign minister.

In his memoir, *The Accidental President of Brazil,* Cardoso relates how he became Finance Minister. He was in New York in May 1993, returning from a trip to Japan, when Itamar called. As Cardoso relates the conversation, Itamar asked " 'Are you sitting down or standing up?' 'Well, I'm sitting now.' 'I was thinking of naming you finance minister,' he said. A shiver ran down my spine. 'Look, Itamar,' I intoned, desperately trying to reason with him. 'We've already talked about this. I told you what I think. I'm perfectly happy in the foreign ministry.' 'I know,' Itamar said. 'But it's not me that needs you. It's Brazil.' "[1]

Cardoso thought he was off the hook, but Itamar made the decision and it appeared in the *Diario Oficial* the next morning in Brasília. He was the new finance minister. In his memoir, he poignantly states that "there were two dirty little secrets of Brazilian inflation, and this was one of them: it benefited a great many people. Among the biggest winners, in fact, were the politicians."[2] Well known to most analysts, the political class enjoyed printing money. It made everyone happy—in the short term. The "second dirty little secret was that the poor in Brazil were the ones most punished by inflation. For decades, no one in Brazil wanted to acknowledge this."[3] As Cardoso indicated, the poor could not benefit from the many schemes that allowed the wealthy to avoid the harshest impact of inflation—indexed bank accounts and similar tools. Cardoso wrote that "we needed more than just an inflation plan. We needed to reinvent Brazil."[4]

Cardoso clearly was the architect of modern Brazil. His leadership—and courage—in confronting the entrenched economic and political powers in Brazil did indeed reinvent the country. One could say that 1994 was the opening phase of the new Brazil and it was the hard work and insight of Fernando Henrique Cardoso that made it happen. As he commented, "my presidency was, at its most basic level, about trying to turn Brazil into a stable country."[5]

Was the Plano Real *(Real Plan) for real?*

Cardoso quickly assembled a team of young, enthusiastic economists to draft what would become the anti-inflation program, the Real Plan. He commented in his memoir, "My main responsibility was to make them keep things simple. I kept telling them, 'I'm the poor guy who's going to have to sell this plan on television, so if I don't understand what you're talking about, then something is definitely wrong.' "[6]

Working around the clock, and keeping the president in the dark, they assembled a simple but effective program. In June, the team announced an "immediate action plan." It called for a US$6 billion cut in government spending. It also called for tightening tax collection and for addressing the chronic issue of the indebted state governments who were always bailed out by Brasília. This program was the first sign that the new team at the finance ministry meant business. The full program was announced in December 1993. Originally met with skepticism, after so many failed plans, this time it worked. There were three main components to the plan. The first was a new currency, the *real*. As Cardoso states in his memoir, it means "royal" and had been used in the colonial era, signaling that the new currency was part of Brazilian history. The name was also used to convince the Brazilian people that its value would be real and not ephemeral like so many of the "new" currencies used after 1985. Second, the plan called for further deep budget cuts to be implemented through a "Social Emergency Fund" that was approved by the Congress. It ceded about US$15 billion of earmarked government spending to the finance ministry. It was a mechanism to give the currency real value, to slow inflation, and create confidence in the ability of the government to maintain the program. It called for listing prices in stores in the old and the new currency, over six months. Slowly, people would understand the true value of the new currency and the country would be free from the curse of constant indexation. By March 1994, the first steps of the new plan were in place; the new currency would be launched a few months later—in the middle of the presidential campaign for the October 3, 1994 presidential election.

Cardoso versus Lula—Did the right man win in 1994?

As the country slowly came to the realization that the Real Plan had changed their lives for the better, presidential politics took front and center. The "obvious" candidate was Lula of the Workers Party (PT). He had narrowly lost to Collor de Melo in a second round in 1989. In mid-1994 he was the front runner by a large margin in the polls. This was the old, cantankerous Lula, anti-capitalist, anti-establishment, anti-anything that didn't conform to the doctrinaire policies of the party. He actually advocated defaulting on the country's foreign debt and the nationalization of the banking sector.

Cardoso decided to throw his hat in the ring in large part to be sure the Real Plan remained in place. Inexorably, as inflation continued to fall, his standing in the polls rose. In September 1964, prices rose just 1.51 percent. On October 3, Cardoso won in the first round with 54 percent of the votes cast; Lula received 27 percent. Clearly, his anti-Real campaign had failed. Brazilians understood the meaning of no/low inflation. The PT appeared stuck in the past—or in the mud. The people had spoken and the intellectual sociologist from São Paulo, from a privileged family, was now the president of Brazil.

What did the first Cardoso administration achieve?

Reform in Brazil has always been an uphill battle. Congressional interests were usually not complementary to that of the president. State and municipal politics, often played out through the congressional delegation from the states, were influential. State governors, in particular, were powerful veto players at times. Since Brazil is a multiparty system, there is never a majority party. Constant coalition-building was—and is—necessary. One of the first priorities of the new government was to continue with the program of privatizing state companies. This process had begun slowly under Collor de Mello. Itamar reluctantly continued the program but it was only after 1995 that the privatization effort accelerated. In the first term, the Cardoso government brought in US$73.4 billion in revenue. The left was unsupportive; there was litigation; political forces in those states where the companies were located were opposed, given that jobs would be lost. Interestingly, workers were often allowed to bid for shares in the privatized companies and this often set them against the powerful unions. Foreign investors found Brazil an attractive place in which to invest. Brazil became more competitive and more open to foreign direct investment as a result of the program.

Other key areas in which the government was successful were in passing an amendment to the Constitution to open up oil exploration and production to domestic and international private capital; a new law established an entity to improve the financial state of the social security system; another law set new rates of social insurance contributions for active and inactive public servants; a number of state banks were privatized to preclude their failing; an insurance scheme to guarantee individual bank deposits was approved; legislation passed Congress to support the restructuring and strengthening of the banking system; the telecommunications industry was liberalized to allow both Brazilian and foreign companies to provide telephone and data transmission services under license from the federal government; and the tax system was simplified but still remains a major hindrance to more rapid growth.

Trade liberalization, which had begun under Collor de Mello, was a major change in the Cardoso years. As one commentator has noted:

> Liberalization was structured to stay and entrepreneurs had to respond. Productivity change is pro-cyclical, and in Brazil at that time even more so. Tariff reductions were seen as permanent. Firms adjusted by shedding workers and modernizing. There was a focus on introducing new technology, as occurred in the automobile sector. Many smaller firms, unable to cope, went out of business.[7]

On the social side, the Cardoso administration inherited the serious problem of AIDS. The infection rate in Brazil was the highest in Latin America. The healthcare system, never robust, was overwhelmed. The number of cases continued to increase. The campaign focused on the use of condoms. In 1996, Congress passed a new law that guaranteed Brazilians free access to antiviral drugs—but they were very expensive to purchase for the average patient. The government encouraged Brazilian drug firms to make cheaper, generic versions of the foreign medications that weren't protected under local patents. For the drugs covered by patents, the administration lobbied the companies to reduce the price. The drug companies reacted with sharp protests. But the Cardoso government built a coalition of NGOs, the public, the scientific community, and United Nations agencies. The United States had joined the fight when it presented a complaint before the World Trade Organization (WTO) stipulating that the policy violated established international property rights laws. After some years of public opinion moving to support Brazil, the United States withdrew the complaint. While AIDS continues to be a major health challenge in Brazil, the Cardoso government valiantly fought and won a battle in the long war against the disease.

One of the major disappointments of the first term was the inability to introduce deeper fiscal reform. The public sector payroll was a major obstacle. Employment in the public sector was the backbone of politics in Brazil. The workers were well organized and vocal and they voted at election time. The government also failed in its efforts to reform the civil service pension system. As a result, pension expenditures climbed from 35 to 43 percent of total public-sector personnel expenditures between the end of 1992 and the late 1990s. The federal government was obligated by the 1988 Constitution to transfer significant resources to the state and municipal governments, further putting pressure on the federal budget.

As always in Brazil, politics drives the policy process. The 1988 Constitution gave the president only one four-year term of office. As the success of the Real Plan became obvious, the presidential palace decided to open negotiations to amend the constitution to allow Cardoso to seek a second term. This had probably unintended consequences for the fiscal situation. To achieve a majority in Congress the president had to agree to allow governors and mayors to seek a second term and it required the expenditure of a great deal of money throughout the system to win support. The amendment was approved in June 1997 but at a high fiscal cost.

There is no doubt that the 1994 election in Brazil produced the right national leader. While the president often said he was, at times, more of a sociologist than a politician, he provided new standards of public conduct and he assembled a talented group of ministers to move the modernization agenda forward. Much was achieved but much was left to be done.

Could Brazil have avoided the default of January 1999?

While the administration was involved in day-to-day challenges from domestic political forces, the external environment became less benign. The first sign of global stress was the unexpected devaluation of the Mexican peso in December 1994. The US government and the international financial institutions reacted and provided immediate support for Mexico. The so-called "tequila effect" had an immediate impact on developing economies. Brasília reacted quickly because the economy was vulnerable due to its overvalued currency and large current account deficit. The Real was devalued quickly and the central bank adopted a crawling peg: frequent but unpredictable small devaluations of the currency that increased the flexibility of the exchange rate regime. It was also decided to increase interest rates.

As a result of these policies, inflation remained under control from 1995 to 1998. But in the latter year the federal government's primary balance (that excludes interest payments on debt) moved from surplus to deficit. The principal reason was the continued hiring of public-sector workers. To balance the budget, the government was forced to go increasingly into debt. The situation also created a persistent current account deficit. The deficit was financed through continued flows of foreign capital and increased domestic and foreign debt. As the current account deficit increased, the interest rate differentials in favor of the Brazilian market had to rise to continue to attract inflows of foreign capital. Higher interest rates reduced economic activity, increased the costs of servicing outstanding debt payments, and caused a rapid expansion in the ratio of public debt to GDP.

In 1997–1998 Brazil was in a reasonably solid economic situation. International reserves were in the range of $55 billion to $60 billion dollars. Brazil remained an attractive location for foreign direct investment. But the inability to deepen the fiscal reform program proved to be a vulnerability as the global context changed dramatically. The Asian financial crisis began when the government of Thailand abruptly devalued the baht on July 2, 1997, allowing the currency to float. Contagion quickly occurred and the crisis spread across Asia impacting vulnerable economies. At first it appeared that the situation would be controlled by the intervention of the US government and the international financial institutions. But as the crisis deepened confidence in emerging market economies weakened. Brazil's reserves began to fall. The authorities raised interest rates and tightened fiscal policy; those measures appeared to stabilize the economy by the end of 1997. But the situation worsened in the summer of 1998 when Russia defaulted on its external debt and devalued the ruble. International finance reacted negatively to the crisis surrounding a major US investment fund, Long-Term Capital Management, leading to a sharp decrease in liquidity in global capital markets. Brazilian reserves continued to fall. Foreign direct investors decided to reduce their exposure to countries like Brazil. To try and keep investors in the marketplace, the government raised interest rates; they were nearly at 50 percent by September 1998. But investors saw the risk as too high to continue to invest in Brazil.

In the midst of the growing financial uncertainty, the president was reelected with 53.1 percent of the vote in the October 1998 election; Lula placed a distant second. Cardoso's government proposed to Congress a fiscal adjustment program, but Congress was not interested in fiscal cuts to some of their favorite programs. As a sign of confidence in the Cardoso government, the United States, the International Monetary Fund (IMF), and the World Bank put together a rescue package of $41.5 billion in November 1998. The president tried again to convince Congress of the high priority of the reforms. While a few bills were passed, the major issue of social security reform was rejected. By mid-January, the financial authorities admitted defeat and allowed the currency to float to meet market expectations. A change in the leadership of the Central Bank in early 1999 began to restore confidence in the policies of the government but without congressional action on proposed cost-cutting measures.

Could Brazil have followed a different policy path?

Following the devaluation in January 1999 there was a great deal of speculation regarding earlier, preventive measures that the government could have taken. Albert Fishlow has written that earlier action, in 1996–1997, by Congress to lower the deficit might have precluded the 1999 devaluation. Lowering interest rates might have stimulated domestic buying and smaller capital inflows might have reduced pressure on the currency. But none of these policies were implemented.

As the government came to grips with the new realities, the macroeconomic program changed. As Fishlow comments, a new "macroeconomic trinity" was introduced.[8] This included inflation targeting, a floating exchange rate, and openness to foreign capital inflow. The new approach yielded relatively rapid and positive results. The current account deficit fell; inflation was reduced; and interest rates declined. An important benchmark was set with the approval of a Law of Fiscal Responsibility in May 2000. This landmark legislation eliminated public sector deficits and restricted access to future indebtedness.[9] Some progress was made on introducing budgetary discipline in the final years of the administration.

But the remaining years of the second Cardoso term were lackluster. Lower rainfall led to rationing and a negative reaction by the public to shortages. The Argentine economy collapsed at the end of 2001, which resulted in a sharp drop in Brazilian exports to its neighbor, the country's third-largest export market. The US economy entered into recession in 2001, further reducing the country's export opportunities. The United States was the largest market, at the time, for Brazilian exports. Global financial markets reacted negatively to the terrorist attack on the United States on September 11, 2001, creating volatility and uncertainty in capital flows to developing countries.

The eight years of the Cardoso government can be neatly, if sadly, divided into two periods. The first term saw impressive progress on restructuring the economy—even if the fiscal situation was never fully addressed. The second four years were a period of reaction to the dramatic events of late 1998 and early 1999. While the central bank was an efficient manager of the country's accounts, a full recovery never took place. The government should be given credit for the slow recovery after the devaluation but externalities intervened, as did the general expectation that, again, it was time for a change of leadership for the new century.

6

THE LULA GOVERNMENT

AN ASSESSMENT

The 2002 national campaign took place in the context of continued economic uncertainty. The Social Democrats nominated a close associate of Cardoso from São Paulo, José Serra. Unsurprisingly, Lula was the candidate of the opposition PT:

> Lula campaigned in 2002 explicitly against the market-oriented, neoliberal economic reforms embraced by his predecessor, Fernando Henrique Cardoso (PSDB, Social Democratic Party of Brazil). His opposition to these market-oriented reforms resonated among Brazilians, many of whom had become disenchanted with the course of economic policy under Cardoso.[1]

Public opinion suggested that practically any national candidate would defeat Serra, who attempted to distance himself from the policies of the outgoing administration. But to no avail.

Lula's election was a landslide—61.43 percent of the vote; Serra received 38.57 percent.

A more pragmatic Lula emerged during the campaign in contrast to his "old" image as a metalworker with little sophistication and little understanding of international finance. In June 2002 the candidate released his *carta ao povo brasileiro* (Letter to the Brazilian people). In that document, he clearly stated that his government would honor all of the country's debts, contracts, and other outstanding financial obligations. Indeed, quietly, and over the fierce resistance of the more radical members of the PT, he began to reach out to the business community in the mid-1990s to understand their concerns and expectations from a PT government. He also chose a conservative businessman as his running mate to assure that constituency that he would indeed honor the promises that he made in the letter to the Brazilian people.

The PT also issued a policy paper prior to the elections that set out the basic outlines of the government's economic program. It "explicitly stated the need to promote rapid economic growth and international competitiveness as a backdrop to achieving social development."[2] There were six policy priorities in the document: price stability, efficiency of the tax system, provisions of long-term finance, investment in research and development, education of the workforce, and selective investments in infrastructure. Addressing poverty and inequality remained central goals of the PT, but by 2002 cooler heads in the party had decided that a pragmatic, transparent approach would be needed after the elections.

Lula's side of the PT had also come to realize that

> if the capital markets had decided Brazil was insolvent, the resulting pressure on the real and domestic interest rates would guarantee that Brazil would, in fact, be insolvent. If capital markets had decided Brazil was solvent, Brazil would, in fact, have been solvent. The investor community was entirely aware of this role, noting that Lula needed to strongly signal a fiscally conservative orientation so that he could win the game of investor sentiment.[3]

Lula also reconfirmed the pragmatic approach of the new government by appointing Henrique Meirelles, a prominent private banker, as president of the Central Bank. He also indicated that he favored reform of the public-sector pension system, a primary contributor to the continuing fiscal crisis. All of these decisions created a high level of tension between the incoming pragmatic Lula and the ideological rank and file. The situation would continue throughout the first term of office.

By January 2003 the stage was set for the new president to continue to assure global investors and the markets in general that this was the "real deal." The old rhetoric was just that. Brazil was about to begin an extraordinary period of growth; but a strong commitment to introduce needed structural reforms was missing. Lula proved to be an extremely charismatic leader and, as always in politics, lucky, as we shall see.

Who is Lula?

Fernando Henrique Cardoso nicely summarized his adversary's background in his memoir:

> The sixth of twenty-three children born to a farmer in the impoverished Northeastern state of Pernambuco, Lula had it rough from the very beginning. He was the only one of his siblings to finish primary school. As a young child, he sold peanuts, tapioca, and oranges on the streets after his family moved to the industrial suburbs of São Paulo to seek work. The family lived in a tiny apartment in the back of a bar, and they had to share a bathroom with the tavern's customers. It was then, Lula later recalled, that he first realized that his family was poor. As a teenager, Lula found a job in a factory producing screws. Working the late shift one night, he was replacing a nut on a machine while a colleague held down the brake. His colleague nodded off, and the blade on the machine slipped forward, cutting off the little finger on Lula's left hand. By the time Lula turned eighteen, he was already a grizzled member of the country's emerging working class.[4]

Lula became politicized during the military dictatorship. He became a leader in the metalworkers union in the industrial suburbs of São Paulo. The union was critical to the expanding auto industry in Brazil. Lula refused to follow the rules of the game in labor negotiations as defined and controlled by the military regime. He bypassed the federation run by the government and took union grievances to the union courts. The threat of intervention by the court forced the auto companies to begin granting concessions to the union. In the late 1970s, the dictatorship faced widespread strikes for the first time. Lula was front and center in rallying the troops. When the labor court ruled again in favor of the union demands, surprisingly, he decided to continue the strike. Shortly thereafter, Lula was forced out of the union and arrested. As the dictatorship moved to an unpredictable end, Lula, freed from prison, organized the workers and created the Workers Party (PT), which quickly became known as the only "modern" political party in Brazil. Lula continued to be a forceful spokesman for worker rights and increasingly for government action against poverty and injustice. He campaigned for the presidency three times before his impressive victory in the election of 2002. He remains one of the most popular politicians in Brazil and was a major figure in the 2010 and 2014 election campaigns of his successor, Dilma Rousseff.

Was Lula prepared to govern in 2003?

As we have seen, Lula understood the precarious nature of the Brazilian economy as he assumed office. He recognized the necessity of accepting fiscal discipline and avoiding any hint of recklessness in economic policymaking. Immediately after entering the presidential palace in Brasília, he raised the 2003 primary surplus from 3.75 percent to 4.25 percent of GDP. In 2004, the primary surplus reached 4.7 percent of GDP. Taxes were increased and revenues were tightly controlled. Interest rates remained relatively high in 2003. While growth was modest in 2003, it accelerated in 2004. In large part this increase was caused by the rapid growth in exports that created a positive trade balance. At the same time, the current account turned positive in 2003. It was clear midway through Lula's first administration that good policies were producing growth with stability.

While the government maintained careful control of its finances, it deliberately sought ways to address poverty in Brazil. The principal mechanism was a series of innovations known as Conditional Cash Transfer (CCT) programs. Brazil had begun to experiment with these innovative policies under President Cardoso but they were limited by the difficult economic circumstances the country faced after the 1999 devaluation. A basic income program was created at the municipal level in 1994.

Other initiatives followed and very quickly the CCT concept became popular with the more disadvantaged segment of the population, as well as with politicians. There was a School "Bolsa" and a Nutrition Bolsa under Cardoso. These programs transferred resources directly to the municipalities in the poorest areas of the country. But all of the initiatives had "conditions" attached. For example, the Nutrition Bolsa was directed to reduce nutritional deficiencies and infant mortality, widespread across the poorest regions. The cash transfer required, for example, women to schedule regular prenatal care, vaccination appointments, and health education. The CCT concept was a major issue in the 2002 campaign, with each side promising to do more for the poor, if elected.

Lula created a Ministry for Food Security; the showcase was a Zero Hunger program. Families that earned less than one-half the minimum wage received a food bonus distributed by a debit card. An innovative part of the program was that the card was sent to the mothers in the poor families on the assumption that they would be more likely to follow the conditions. It became clear to the Lula government that there were overlapping and often competing government offices trying to serve as the principal sponsor of the programs. Lula then created one Ministry for Social Development in January 2004 to coordinate all of the various poverty reduction schemes. The key component of the new initiative was *Bolsa Familia* (Family Package), created in October 2003. This proved to be a cornerstone of the Lula government and brought tens of millions of poor Brazilians into the market for the first time. It also began to address the long-standing marginalization of the poor in Brazilian society and at relatively low cost.

Another important policy innovation of the Lula administration was social security reform. Draft legislation was submitted to the Congress and approved in December 2003. The minimum retirement age for civil servants was increased; retired civil servants were required to contribute to the social security system if their income was above an established amount; limitations were put in place on the amount of pensions paid to widows and orphans of civil servants; caps were initiated on civil servants' wages and retirement benefits; a maximum cap on the size of the civil service was mandated; and a cap on pensions received by private sector retirees was legislated. But as Albert Fishlow has commented, "future adjustments remain necessary. Delay has a calculable price: the longer the country waits, the more drastic the change that will be required." And he continues, "Brazil has developed a pension system that is sui generis: quite substantial in magnitude and dependent upon extensive public subsidy but hardly equalizing . . . the net welfare effect is negative."[5]

While the record of the first Lula administration was considered reasonably successful, a major scandal erupted in June 2005. The *Mensalão*—or large monthly payment—scandal revealed that the PT government had paid a number of members of Congress a monthly stipend to vote for the government's legislative program. Suddenly, it became clear why the Lula government had done so well in passing legislation. Members of Congress resigned as did senior officials in the executive branch. While there were rumors of President

Lula's involvement, nothing was proven. He denied any knowledge of the illegal activities. He became known in the popular jargon as the "teflon" president. The scandal uncovered what was widely known—the multiparty system was dysfunctional. Every president had to build coalitions vote by vote. Various "veto players" had to be persuaded to support the administration. Money was plentiful and its distribution was relatively easy. The system may well have continued if a "whistle-blower" in Congress had not revealed the existence of the program.

As the first Lula administration ended in 2006, Werner Baer stated the following:

> It remained faced with a fundamental dilemma: the need to simultaneously maintain economic respectability within a globalized international financial system while attempting to remedy the country's grave socioeconomic disparities ... the recent experience of Brazil suggests that the simultaneous achievement of macroeconomic stability and socioeconomic change can be problematic. The alternative possibility of adopting a sequential approach in which a period of economic orthodoxy precedes a period of growth and redistribution which may appear a reasonable path was shown also in the case of Brazil to be problematic.[6]

In spite of the monthly payment scheme, Lula proved to be a deft political leader during his first term of office. He was charismatic and communicative. He was also lucky as we shall see.

Are the BRICS for real?

As the transition from Cardoso to Lula was taking place, Goldman Sachs, the prominent investment firm in New York, published a research paper in 2001 entitled "The World Needs Better Economic BRICs" (South Africa would be added later to create the "S"). Thus the acronym that became famous—or infamous—was born. Global Economics Paper No: 99 (October 1, 2003) stated the following:

> Over the next 50 years, Brazil, Russia, India and China—the BRICs economies—could become a much larger force in the world economy. . . if things go right, in less than forty years, the BRICs economies together could be larger than the G6 in U.S. dollar terms. By 2025 they could account for over half the size of the G6. Of the current G6, only the United States and Japan may be among the six largest economies in US dollar terms in 2050.[7]

The report, which triggered a firestorm of controversy, went on to say that Brazil's GDP growth would average 3.6 percent over the next fifty years, overtaking the size of Italy's economy by 2025, France's by 2031, and the UK's and Germany's by 2036.[8]

The analysts did caution that Brazil faced challenges in meeting the targets laid out by Goldman Sachs. These included the need to open to trade; increase investment and savings; and reduce public and foreign debt, which would require a deep fiscal adjustment and a lower debt-to-GDP ratio. In addition, they set forth a set of core factors—macroeconomic stability, institutional capacity, openness, and education—as conditions for growth. We will return to the last of those factors—education—that will indicate that Brazil is making little progress in implementing an innovative education policy.

But a sense of euphoria set in. President Lula became the BRIC president. As we have seen, Brazilian exports soared during his presidency. Demand for commodities and raw materials, goods that Brazil has in abundance, exploded, especially from China. But in the Global Economics Paper No: 134 (December 2005) there was a cautionary note that the Lula government chose to ignore. The Paper said that "Brazil scored relatively well on measures of political stability, life expectancy and technology adoption but quite poorly on investment, education levels, openness to trade, and government deficit."[9] These comments would be repeated in other Sachs research papers throughout the decade.

But high levels of growth, soaring foreign direct and portfolio investment, a decision to abandon its understanding with the IMF, and related developments led the Lula government to applaud its progress and to avoid the hard political decisions. In another paper, published in December 2006, on the eve of Lula's second term of office, entitled "The 'B' in BRICs: Unlocking Brazil's Growth Potential," Goldman analysts stated that "Brazil has underperformed not only relative to our expectations but also compared with all the other BRICs. Since 2003, real GDP growth rates in China, India, and Russia have averaged 10.2 percent, 8.0 percent and 6.9 percent in each case, far exceeding our estimates of their long-term potential (4.9 percent, 5.8 percent, and 3.5 percent respectively)."[10] The report commented that since the 2003 paper was issued, Brazil has grown only at a disappointing 2.7 percent on average, compared with the 3.7 percent that they had estimated its long-term growth potential to be. Presciently, the report stated that: "We do not believe that the Lula II administration and Congress will be ambitious enough to implement this politically difficult agenda. Therefore, while Brazil has the potential to grow at or above five percent this is unlikely to happen during the next four years."[11]

The emergence of the BRICs also set-off a wide-ranging debate about the appropriate role of those countries in world governance. Brazil became a vocal participant in this debate. Writing in the *Financial Times*, Jim O'Neill of Goldman Sachs said that "it is imperative that western leaders encourage more rapid institutional changes to the structure of G7, G8, IMF, and world governance bodies."[12] This, of course, was shortly before the beginning of the global financial crisis and the collapse of Lehman Brothers on September 15, 2008. The call for broader participation by the BRICs was a popular notion during Lula's second administration. After the crisis began, Brazil was front and center in efforts to contain the crisis by working diligently to revive the G-20 (the twenty largest economies in the world) that had fallen into near irrelevancy. Lula was fond of saying that Brazil was the last important country to go into the crisis and first to emerge relatively unscathed. As we will see, the good days were ending for Brazil in 2008–2009 and the years of very slow growth were to begin under the next government in 2010.

But the BRICS have survived. They hold annual meetings: the 2014 meeting was held in Fortaleza, Brazil, where the five leaders announced that they were establishing a development bank to challenge the Bretton Woods institutions—the IMF and the World Bank—created after World War II at a conference in New Hampshire. The new bank will be based in Shanghai and India will name the first president. The leaders also said that they would create a $100 million fund of currency reserves for the members to use during balance of payments crises.

There is skepticism among the industrial countries, as might be expected. The venerable IMF and World Bank have been the backbone of economic and financial policy for seventy years. Yet, as the *Financial Times* commented, following the Fortaleza summit, "the Bretton Woods institutions reflect the realities of a receding age. The world has changed, mostly for the better, as poor countries close the gap on rich ones. The BRICS bank encapsulates this. It is a glimpse of the future."[13]

Part of the motivation to create the new institutions is the failure of the industrial nations to reform the voting policies of the IMF. The BRICS now represent more than a fifth of global output and almost half of the world's population, but have just 10.3 percent of the voting rights; European countries are allocated 27.5 percent of voting rights and now represent only 18 percent of output. The BRICS also resent the fact that the leadership of the IMF is "reserved" for a European and the World Bank for an American. Reforms were negotiated in 2010 to give six percentage points—not enough—to the developing countries, but the US Congress refused to ratify the agreement.

The BRICS also encapsulate the resentment in the developing world over the autocratic policymaking process at the IMF. During the crises of the late 1990s, the Fund imposed punishing policies that caused grave economic and social hardship. The new funding will allow the BRICS, at least, to avoid that draconian approach to reform. Brazil will remain an important player in the world of the BRICS even if its current state of low growth continues for a while. It has become an important part of the country's foreign policy, as will be discussed at a later point in this book.

Was Lula's second term (2005–2010) as good as it gets?

There was a dramatic shift in the popular base for Lula's reelection in 2006. In 2002, the votes came mainly from the south and southeast, the more developed regions of the country. The poor states of the northeast and north were still controlled by local political bosses, all conservative, and fearful of the socialist tinge of the PT platform. They were content with the status quo. *Bolsa Família* changed that. In just three to four years, tens of millions felt that the Lula government had governed in their favor; the south and southeast felt they were not the beneficiaries of the PT regime. In 2006, Lula was forced into a second round but defeated the governor of the state of São Paulo with 60.8 percent of the national vote.

In addition to the BRICs publicity, the first years of the second mandate were exciting. On April 30, 2008, Standard and Poor's was the first rating agency to designate Brazil as one of fourteen sovereign states with an investment grade rating (BBB or higher) for its foreign currency debt. The report noted that:

> The upgrades reflect the maturation of Brazil's institutions and policy framework, as evidenced by the easing of fiscal and external debt burdens and improved trend growth projects. While net general government debt remains higher than that in many "BBB" peers, a fairly

> predictable trace record of pragmatic fiscal and debt management policies mitigates this risk.[14]

Fitch Ratings was next on June 3, 2008, commenting that:

> The rating upgrade reflects the dramatic improvement in Brazil's external and public sector balance sheet that has greatly reduced Brazil's vulnerability to external and exchange rate shocks and entrenched macroeconomic stability and enhanced medium-term growth prospects. The authorities have established a track record of commitment to low inflation and a primary budget surplus that has dispelled previous concerns over medium-term fiscal sustainability. Brazil's investment-grade ratings are also supported by its diverse, high value-added economy . . . and its relative political and social stability.[15]

Moody's and Dominion Bond Rating Service followed shortly thereafter. Investors were delighted and money poured into the country.

The second term also saw the establishment of the Program for Accelerated Growth (PAC) in 2007. The PAC emphasized physical infrastructure, energy, and a social and urban commitment in the areas of housing, sewerage facilities, and related necessities. In March 2010, Lula announced PAC II. Both have been disappointing. Critics say that lack of coordination, alleged corruption, conflicting goals between the federal government and the states and municipalities, and the frustrating and cumbersome regulatory framework are to blame.

The years of good growth and high expectations

The final jewel in the crown of the B in BRICs occurred in the energy field. It was often commented in the Lula years that God had to be a Brazilian, given the impressive strides the country had made since the 2002 election—export-led growth, investment grade ratings, the PACs (in their earlier stage of implementation), social security and tax reforms. What was next? Petroleum. In 2007–2008, Petrobras, the state oil company, began to discover massive petroleum and natural gas reserves deep under water and under a thick layer of salt. With colorful names like Tupi and Jupiter, Lula called the oil find the second independence of Brazil. Brazil had reached self-sufficiency in 2006. The new discoveries offered the prospects for total independence and for the country to become an oil giant with massive proven reserves. Unfortunately, the bonanza has become something of a bust. As we will see in the section on the Dilma Rousseff government (2011–2014), Petrobras has been overtly politicized. The major global oil companies have been reluctant to invest. Ongoing disputes over the distribution of the oil revenues have slowed development—most of the finds are off the southeast coast but the rest of the federation believes it deserves to share in the wealth. It remains to be seen if the next government will be able to find the political will to change the terms of engagement for the global oil companies and to reduce the local content burden and the manipulation of domestic petroleum prices to allow the company to return to competitiveness.

Lula was lucky. The good years carried him to the end of his second administration. He was able to choose his successor and successfully secure her election on the PT ticket. There were foreign policy differences with the United States that we will review later, but the president refused to consider changing the constitution to run for a third term and retired with high levels of popularity—and that continues to this day. But Lula was not a born reformer. He was a shrewd, streetsmart politician who liked to please. To do so meant going along to get along politically. The tough reforms were pushed forward. The good years hid the faults that we have discussed. It would be to his successor to confront the long-neglected agenda that Goldman Sachs had highlighted in a number of reports.

Why does Brazil not take education seriously?

It is generally acknowledged that education is intricately tied to productivity and competitiveness. But Brazil apparently has not received the message. The World Economic Forum (WEF) ranked 148 countries in its "Global Competitiveness Index (GCI-2013-2014)" and Brazil stood at 56, down from 48 the year before, and 53 two years ago. The country ranked 129th in terms of the quality of primary education in the Index. In the "pillar" of higher education and training, it qualified at 136th in quality of math and science education; the overall position of the quality of the education system stood at 121st. Under the "pillar" of innovation, Brazil was ranked at 112th in terms of the availability of scientists and engineers. The Forum commented that Brazil's low ranking was due to an insufficient degree of competition and gaps in terms of education and training, technology, and innovation that prevent many companies from moving to higher-value-added activities.[16]

The Getúlio Vargas Foundation's (GVF) *The Brazilian Economy* publication devoted an issue to education in 2014. In the "From the Editors" page it was starkly stated that "education ties with infrastructure as the main problem holding Brazil back."[17] Interestingly, the World Economic Forum's GCI reported that inadequate supply of infrastructure was the first ranked in "the most problematic factors for doing business" in the country). The GVF report commented that "the current curriculum is rigidly outdated, incapable of promoting innovation and adaptation to technological progress."[18] Today, over 8.5 million primary and secondary students are at least two years behind the grade level for their age, high school dropouts are very numerous, and high school students in Brazil have few options for vocational training. The report continues to comment that "poor education limits student work opportunities, creates mismatches between worker skills and company needs, and thus stifles productivity."[19]

One of the mismatches that plagues Brazilian education is the fact that Brazil spent, in 2011, on average, US$10,000 per college student in high-quality free public universities—almost five times what it spends on students in basic education. For decades the upper class has been able to afford to send their children to quality private primary and secondary schools that qualify them to pass the entrance examination for the public universities. Less fortunate children attend public primary and secondary schools—and cannot pass the entrance exam. If they continue their education at the university level—most do not—they attend inadequate private universities, usually at night, and pay tuition.

The US Conference Board reported in 2013 that average earnings for Brazilians were US$10.80 an hour, the lowest among Latin American countries (compared to US$20.80 in Chile, US$16.80 in Mexico, and US$13.90 in Argentina). The director general of the National Service of Industrial Learning (SENAI) and director of Education and Technology of the National Confederation of Industry (CNI) stated in the GVF report that "it takes three Brazilian workers to produce as much as one South Korean, four as much as one German, and five as much as one American."[20] We have very clear productivity deficiencies we must address, he stated. One analyst said that "to reach even half of US productivity Brazil would have to increase productivity growth from the current 1 percent to about 2–2.5 percent." And that will take forty years, he concluded.[21]

The GVF report indicates a number of areas that desperately need improvement in the country's education system. Front and center is good management that requires planning. The country needs to expand vocational technical education. To its credit, the government in 2011 launched the National Program for Access to Technical Education and Employment (Pronatec) to expand access to vocational education. An excellent initiative, but one interviewee in the GVF report commented that the skills taught in high school should be those the economy needs. The GVF report further comments:

> Today, we have almost no idea whether regions, states, or the country itself offers the courses the labor market requires. This is a serious gap. It is clear that teachers need better training and pay. The Congress passed the National Salary Floor for Teachers Law in 2008 but many states and municipalities lack the resources to comply. The quality of teachers in Brazil is low. In Brazil only twenty-five percent of instructors have completed a teacher-education course; the world average is ninety percent.[22]

One of the major shortcomings in the education system in Brazil is that it is the states and municipalities that control the system. Brasília is directly responsible for funding the public universities but it does provide some resources and sets national standards. The state and local governments vary in levels of competence and the degree of commitment to education in general. Money does not seem to be the major problem—how it is spent is the issue. Currently, Brazil spends 6 percent of GDP on education—about the average for the OECD countries.

The new National Education Plan (PNE), approved in May 2014, will raise that to 10 percent over ten years. There is concern among education reformers that much of that money will be spent wastefully. One new initiative, the Science Without Borders Program, approved in 2011, provides scholarships for students to study abroad. But questions have been raised as to whether or not it has been properly evaluated and whether the overseas experience will be incorporated into the country's engineering schools. A recent study by the World Bank on teachers—"Great Teachers: How to Raise Student Learning in Latin America and the Caribbean"—confirms that the region's teachers spent less than 65 percent of their time in class actually teaching—Brazil is in that category—compared with a benchmark of good practice in schools in the US of 85 percent. The rest of the time was spent on administration or simply wasted.[23] There is a growing consensus that targeting teachers for training is a good use of the funds. Bonuses for good performance are another area in which funds could be well used. Financial incentives to become a teacher may be worth considering. The World Bank report states very clearly that teachers "are increasingly recognized as the critical actors in the region's efforts to improve education quality and results."[24] As the WEF report on competitiveness clearly indicates, Brazil lags far behind. The GVF study confirms that conclusion. Brazil's political leaders need to prioritize public education—and do so quickly if the country is not to fall farther behind in terms of productivity and its ability to compete in a global economy.

7

DILMA ROUSSEFF

THE RIGHT CHOICE TO SUCCEED LULA IN 2011?

Unlike many presidents in Latin America, Lula chose to follow the Constitution and not attempt to change it to allow for a third term. In spite of pressure from the PT, he remained firm and it soon became apparent that he had "chosen" the PT candidate. To some surprise, it was Rousseff, then serving as the president's chief of staff in the presidential palace. She was, in many ways, an unlikely candidate. In contrast to Lula's background, Rousseff was raised in an upper-middle-class family in the city of Belo Horizonte in Minas Gerais.

After a traditional education, she was radicalized by the military takeover in 1964 and decided to join the resistance. She opted for an organization that decided to use violence to destabilize the regime. It is reported that she chose the armed struggle after reading *Revolution Inside the Revolution* by Regis Debray, a French intellectual who had settled in Cuba and was a friend of Fidel Castro and his supporters. There is a great deal of speculation as to her role in the revolutionary organizations that were operating at that time. Rousseff argues that she carried out organizational activities; some former colleagues in the movement have said that she was more deeply involved in the operational aspects of the struggle. In January 1970 she was arrested in São Paulo and imprisoned. While in captivity, she was tortured. Released in late 1972, she was expelled from the Federal University of Minas Gerais; she continued her education at the Federal University in RGS, majoring in economics. She and her second husband, Carlos Araujo, decided to remain in Porto Alegre and became involved in activities that challenged the regime but were considered legal.

She became involved in local politics, supporting but not joining the only opposition party permitted at the time, the MDB. When the regime canceled the two-party system and allowed for the formation of new parties, Rousseff first worked with Leonel Brizola, the brother-in-law of President Jango Goulart, in reorganizing the PTB, the Brazilian Workers Party. Brizola was denied the right to resurrect his old political party and established the Democratic Workers Party (PDT). Her first political position was as municipal treasury secretary in Porto Alegre. She later served as the head of a local economics think tank and then as state secretary of energy. She left the PDT after a dispute within the party, and joined Lula's PT. Rousseff became involved in the 2001–2002 presidential campaign, serving as a member of an energy advisory group. After his election, Lula appointed her Minister of Energy. She became a strong advocate for increasing the country's energy capacity, often confronting the Environmental Minister, Marina Silva, who argued that energy development could be an ecological disaster.

When the Lula government became involved in the *Mensalão* scandal, the then chief of staff was forced to resign and Lula asked Rousseff to accept the position. During Lula's second term in office, Lula travelled frequently to reinforce the image of Brazil as an emerging power. One important symbol of that position was Brazil's inclusion in the acronym, BRICS—Brazil, Russia, India, China, and South Africa. In the mid-2000s, these five countries were considered the new, emerging influential states in the global system. Hence it was widely believed that Rousseff handled the day-to-day governance issues in the presidential palace. Rousseff launched her presidential campaign in June 2010 as the official candidate of the PT. Her principal opponent was Governor José Serra of São Paulo. Embracing Lula's policies, and with strong public support from the president, she carried the first round of voting but did not receive 50 percent of the vote, requiring a second round, which she won with 56 percent of the vote. She took office on January 1, 2011.[1]

Were Rousseff's policy dilemmas beyond her control or actually due to her limited political skills?

Unlike lucky Lula, Rousseff inherited an economy with severe challenges. These were easily overlooked during Lula's eight years in the Planalto, with high commodity prices and rising demand for commodities and raw materials. The world economy was robust. Foreign direct investment (FDI) was plentiful—too plentiful, some economists argued. But as Rousseff entered the presidency, the chickens came home to roost. An OECD (Organization of Economic Cooperation and Development) survey in October 2013 previewed the challenges for the Brazilian economy in the years ahead:

> The global crisis has brought shortcomings in productivity and cost competitiveness to the fore. Supply-side constraints, which are increasingly impeding growth, include pressing infrastructure bottlenecks and a high tax burden, exacerbated by an onerous and fragmented tax system. A tight labour market and continuing skill shortages have resulted in strong wage increases. Although credit is rising at a substantial pace, investment financing at longer maturities continues to be scarce. Further development of long-term credit markets is hampered by a lack of private participation, owing to an uneven playing field caused by strong financial support to the national development bank which dominates long-term lending. Brazil's participation in international

> trade and its integration into global production chains is below what would be expected in an economy as large and sophisticated as Brazil's, and domestic producers continue to be shielded from foreign competition.[2]

And an undated OECD report in November 2015 commented that:

> Brazil is now at a turning point. As the tailwinds from high commodity prices have weakened permanently, improving domestic policies will be more important than before.[3]

For any government, in the best of times, this is a daunting agenda. When it might have been possible to address some of these issues—during the Lula presidency—neither the political will nor economic necessity provided the impetus to act. And very little was accomplished in terms of meaningful reform during Rousseff's four years in office.

The OECD report did recognize that there has been wider access to education, but as we discussed previously, the quality remains inferior. Severe shortages in physical school infrastructure are a reality. Students at the secondary level continue to drop out in large numbers and the opportunities for vocational education are very limited. Social expenditures have been heavily focused on pension payments but the report recognized that the conditional cash transfers have been an effective tool to address poverty and inequality. The tax system, in contrast, is characterized by a low degree of progressivity that limits its redistributive impact.

Some of the policy recommendations were well known for some time and were ignored during President Rousseff's first term in office (2010–2014). The need to reduce inflation, spur economic growth with investment, streamline the tax system, and introduce flexible labor legislation were among the most important.

The OECD also recommended that the government reduce the fiscal burden of the pension system by severing the automatic link between pension benefits and the minimum wage by raising effective retirement ages. This of course is a highly controversial and political challenge. As mentioned, physical infrastructure must remain a key policy goal. Reducing tariff protection, to allow competition in the private sector, was a given. The OECD also called for phasing out local content requirements and targeted support to specific sectors of the economy. Another item of concern was rising household indebtedness that in mid-2014 amounted to 44 percent of annual income, including mortgage loans. Debt-service to income ratios of 21 percent exceeded levels in the United States and in many Latin American countries.

The report emphasized that it was important to maintain the three pillars of macroeconomic stability—stable inflation, declining public debt, and a flexible exchange rate. There was widespread concern that the Rousseff government had slipped in its willingness to defend the three pillars. Indeed during the 2014 campaign the press reported that the party said that it had two pillars—consumption, jobs, and wages and income distribution, on the one hand, and social policies on the other. Unfortunately, the rhetoric of the campaign in 2014 did not translate into good policies in 2015–2016. As we shall see, the government was overwhelmed by corruption scandals and a threat to impeach the president that resulted in political deadlock in 2015–2016.

In hindsight, Lula's choice of Rousseff as his successor was probably a mistake. She often appears to dislike politics. She is viewed as a micromanager. Her experience in the energy field has not resulted in good decisions in that policy arena. While it is true that world economic conditions were challenging for the Brazilian government, many argue that better management and policy innovation might have mitigated the worst consequences of the global recession.

Why did the state oil company, Petrobras, underperform during Rousseff's Presidency?

One of the policy issues that has been of great concern to the Rousseff government is the petroleum bonanza discovered in 2007 off the southeast coast. The so-called pre-salt field—the petroleum is in deep water under a thick layer of salt—was heralded as a "game changer" for Brazil—the key to modernization, social inclusion, and a steady income flow. As with many things in Brazil, the discovery was one thing, successful exploitation was another. Petrobras, the state oil company, created by Getúlio Vargas's government in the early 1950s, is a controversial institution. The Rousseff government has been accused of deeply politicizing the company, in particular forcing it to import and sell gasoline at below-market prices, a policy designed to control inflation. Since 2008, the policy has cost the company $20 billion. That lost revenue obligates the company to take on more debt. The company has responded by selling off assets in Peru, Colombia, Africa, and the Gulf of Mexico. Petrobras has also postponed developing other promising oil fields elsewhere in the country.

The government did not address the institutional issues of developing the pre-salt field until 2010, the last year of the Lula administration. Early in that year, Congress passed three of four pieces of legislation: (1) it created a social investment fund to be used for education and health programs; (2) it established a new state-owned oil company, called Pre-Sal Petroleo SA, that will manage the government's pre-salt assets, and; (3) in a complex capitalization plan, the government granted the firm rights to produce five billion barrels of oil from government-held fields. The fourth law, approved in December 2010, granted the federal government greater control over deep water reserves. The new legislation replaced the current concession-based system—favoring the participation of international oil companies—with a production-sharing scheme that increases the role of the state over outside investors and gives Petrobras a minimum 30 percent operating stake in all new subsalt fields. Petrobras will be the operator of the fields under the production-sharing agreements, but other companies will have the right to bid for stakes by guaranteeing the government a large share of the oil that is found. The legislation perversely encumbered the company with huge financial responsibilities and drove away many potential foreign partners.

The new production-sharing agreement does not cover pre-salt areas previously auctioned off under the concession system—which was far more favorable to international oil companies. The agreements also do not affect onshore or shallow-water areas that will be auctioned off under the old concession-based system. Congress also approved a separate law to even out the distribution of royalties among Brazil's twenty-six states and the Federal District of Brasília. This remains highly controversial and it has been difficult to find a formula that addresses the states in the southeast, whose coastlines shadow the deep water oil discoveries.

Responding to sudden widespread rioting in June 2013, the government prioritized new legislation in August that year that designated all royalties from the pre-salt fields to education and health. Seventy-five percent of drilling income will go to education and 25 percent to health programs. The demonstrations began over an unexpected increase in transportation costs but quickly became more about the popular discontent with corruption, poor public schools and health facilities, and the cost of hosting the 2014 World Cup. There has also been a growing sense that the "moment" when pre-salt would have healed all of the country's social and political wounds may have passed. As Juan Forero reported in January 2014, more than six years after the recovery, "The outlook for Brazil's oil industry, much like the Brazilian economy itself, is more sobering. Oil production is stagnant; the state-controlled oil company, Petrobras, is hobbled by debt; and foreign oil companies are wary of investing here."[4]

There are a number of reasons for the new pessimism about the pre-salt. New opportunities have opened in Africa, in the tar sands in Canada, and in shale gas deposits in the United States using fracking—hydraulic fracturing technology. It is also true that while many wells have been drilled in the pre-salt area, many have proven to be dry. Optimistic forecasts by Petrobras officials have been dismissed as unrealistic. The oil company is also burdened with mandates and heavy government interference. For example, to revive the national shipbuilding industry, Petrobras and its partners must use oil platforms and other heavy equipment built domestically; that requirement has resulted in large cost overruns and equipment shortages. This "local content" policy (requiring that domestic firms produce a large percentage of the inputs for the industry) is inefficient and counterproductive, many analysts say. The company held a long-delayed auction for the Libra field (one of the largest pre-salt offshore oil fields) in October 2013 (the first auction since 2008). The winning bid went to a consortium that included Royal Dutch Shell, France's Total, and two Chinese firms. Most startling was the fact that the "majors"—Chevron, BP, and Exxon Mobil—did not participate, and they are the companies with the capital and know-how to develop complex oil basins. It was expected that more than forty companies would participate but only eleven did and not even half of those opted to bid.

Other problems abound. Transport costs are very high because of poor physical infrastructure. Brazilian ports have been overwhelmed and are not up to date. The industry has had serious difficulties in securing qualified workers due to the inadequate supply of engineers and other technical personnel, including vocationally prepared workers, such as welders. The company is also under investigation by Congress for alleged malpractice during the purchase of a refinery in the United States in 2006, when President Rousseff was the Chairwoman of the Board of the company.

And there is another inquiry underway for alleged money laundering. Prosecution documents allege that a convicted black market money dealer and former Petrobras executives created a number of shell companies to skim money from the company and then "wash" it offshore. It is also alleged that the conspirators negotiated with Petrobras contractors to make political donations. The 2014 presidential campaign was dominated to some degree by another scandal linked to kickbacks to political parties and leading politicians; that issue came to define the first years of Rousseff's second term in office and led to calls for her resignation or impeachment by the Congress.

There was some good news for Petrobras in mid-2014 when it was announced that output from the pre-salt fields has passed 500,000 barrels of oil a day, nearly triple that of 2012, and now accounting for a quarter of the company's total production of two million barrels a day. This is very positive news for the company, since production gains in pre-salt fields are essential to offset declines in production in mature fields. Reaching its goal of being among the world's top five global oil producers by 2020 and producing four million barrels a day will require the company to address many or most of the issues raised above.

Is the National Bank for Economic and Social Development (BNDES) too big for its own good?

Founded in June 1952, the BNDES is one of the largest development banks in the world, second to its counterpart in China. The principal reason for its establishment was the need for long-term financing for national development projects. It is funded by a tax on workers as well as recycled loan repayments. But because of a rapid increase in lending, the national treasury now accounts for more than half of BNDES funding, from almost nothing five years ago. The total amount borrowed from the treasury in 2009–2014 was R$386 billion.

Treasury funding is provided at a long-term interest rate known as the TJLP, currently fixed at 5 percent per year. Analysts report that it now lends US$85 billion (190 bn reais) per year "of taxpayers' money at heavily-subsidized negative real interest rates, often to big companies that critics say should be funding themselves on international markets at the same cost as their competitors."[5]

This trend started with the financial crisis of 2008, when the private commercial banks reduced lending out of fear of soaring credit debt. The government then urged the state banks, especially BNDES, to step in. It did so, but critics argue that it favored "national champions" or large corporations. One of the downsides of this policy is that it is a disincentive to corporate lending by private sector banks, preventing the country from developing dynamic and deep capital markets. For most companies private banks are not an option because borrowing costs are prohibitive. In answer to the criticism that the pattern of lending to large firms "crowds out" small and medium-size enterprises, the bank responded that one-third of bank lending in 2013 went to SMEs, compared to one-fifth in 2009.

There is also concern over the possible political implications of lending to large corporations. It has been disclosed that some of the corporations receiving favorable financing from the Bank were very active in contributing to the 2010 and 2014 presidential campaigns of President Rousseff. The lending pattern of the BNDES may not be promoting the growth of small and medium-size businesses in Brazil where many private sector jobs are created.

As another commentator noted:

> If the BNDES provides a solution to what one hopes is a short-term problem—loose fiscal policy and high interest rates—then it also runs the risk of helping to perpetuate that problem. Like a worried parent who funds his children's wayward behavior, it is an enabler.[6]

Assessing whether the Belo Monte Dam project in the Amazon represents a setback for environmental safety—if so, why did the PT support it?

One of the most controversial development projects in Brazilian history is unfolding in the Brazilian Amazon. It is the Belo Monte Dam, the world's third-largest hydroelectric dam; the only larger dams are the Three Gorges in China and Itaipu on the border between Brazil and Paraguay. The dam is under construction on the Xingu River in the state of Pará. Plans for the project began under the military government in 1975, but it was postponed numerous times because of indigenous and environmentalist protests.

The protests in the region date from 1989 when indigenous tribes organized the "First Encounter of the Indigenous Nations of the Xingu." The confrontation between the indigenous people and the Brazilian government drew international attention. A more ambitious plan of the government to build additional dams was shelved. The indigenous leaders argued that the Belo Monte project would cause irreparable harm to the flora and fauna in the river basin and flood about 193 square miles of forest and agricultural land; they argued that 20,000 people would be displaced. Since the project would divert much of the water flow of the Xingu, traditional fishing grounds would be destroyed. Thousands of people would lose access to water, food, and river transportation; rainforests would be submerged; and dead vegetation would rot and release massive amounts of greenhouse gases into the atmosphere.

Following the "Encounter," the project was scaled back. A series of environmental impact assessments was carried out. As a result, further changes were made to divert the water away from indigenous territories. But the indigenous leadership argued that they had not been fully consulted as required in the 1988 Constitution and they organized a second "Encounter" in the city of Altamira, Pará in May 2008. The

Workers Party (PT) decided to proceed with the revised plan and the Brazilian Institute of Environment and Renewable Natural Resources (IBAMA) issued a provisional environmental license, one of three required by Brazilian law for development projects. In April 2010, the Norte Energia consortium won the project auction. In the same month, the federal Attorney General's office suspended the project tender and annulled the provisional environmental license, arguing it was unconstitutional. After further legal maneuvering, President Lula signed the contract with Norte Energia in August 2010. But further bureaucratic dynamics raised the possibility of further postponement. In June 2011, IBAMA issued the full license needed to begin construction. A final legal roadblock was overcome in August 2012 when the Supreme Federal Court gave final approval to continue construction. Rousseff's government strongly supported the Court's decision.

The dam is expected to cost more than $16 billion and the transmission lines another $2.5 billion. Much of the funding has been provided by BNDES—its largest-ever loan. The government justification for the Belo Monte project is that the expanding middle class will need larger amounts of electricity in the future. Failure to plan now could lead to shortages like the ones that occurred in 2001–2002. The government says that the country needs around 6000 megawatts of new electricity generation per year for the next decade to add to its installed generating capacity of 121,000 megawatts.

The United Nations Human Rights Council and the International Labor Organization (ILO) have criticized the government's intention to move forward with the project. Other critics point out that Belo Monte will never generate 11,200 megawatts unless the Xingu River is overflowing. And even then, the rainy season in the Amazon is usually no more than four months a year, between February and May. For the rest of the year, Belo Monte will operate like a mid-sized facility, generating about 40 percent less than its potential. As construction got underway, one report commented the following:

> The area around Belo Monte now looks like another planet. It's barren. It's red. It looks like a huge mining operation, with workers housing erected in neat rows along earthen paths once covered in river water. The area will be inundated again once the dam is ready to function.[7]

Controversial, as well, is the concept of mega-dams. They usually have large cost overruns in local currency terms. And the long-term environmental damage has not been accurately assessed, critics contend. Other analysts argue that Brazil has many energy alternatives. For instance wind power, biomass, possibly shale, and gas are all possibilities. But the Brazilian government has overcome all of the legal challenges and has been able to neutralize indigenous and international opposition to Belo Monte; it will allegedly be finished by 2016.

Will the 2016 Olympics be more successful than the 2014 World Cup Competition?

Brazil won the bid to host the Olympics in October 2009, the first to be held in South America (the losing bids were from Chicago, Madrid, and Tokyo). But the mood in Brazil is decidedly cautious, even pessimistic, particularly after the not-very-successful hosting of the World Cup in 2014. However, compared to the Cup, whose activities were played across the country, the Olympics will take place in and around Rio de Janeiro. The daily focus of the media has been on the slow progress and painful delays in preparing the Cidade Maravilhosa (Marvelous City) for a second major sporting event in two years.

As with the World Cup in 2014, the opening of the games on August 5, 2016 will probably see many of the construction sites unfinished but functional. It is estimated that the Games will attract 10,000 athletes from 206 countries and that poses a challenge to the governments—municipal, state, and federal—that are struggling to coordinate efforts for building permits, environmental endorsements, housing, and public transportation upgrades. There are concerns about security, given a recent wave of robberies and physical attacks on tourists as well as locals.

A major issue that has dominated the press—local and international—is the terrible pollution of beautiful Guanabara Bay that borders Rio de Janeiro's east side and is the host site for the sailing and windsurfing events. The waters are filthy, filled with raw sewage and massive amounts of garbage. Part of Rio's Olympic bid included a promise to clean up the bay by 80 percent, but the government has admitted that they will probably achieve 50 to 55 percent, if all goes according to plan. Medical advisories state that falling into the water, the sailors could potentially be victims of gastrointestinal infections, mycoses, otitis, or hepatitis.

Water is another critical issue in the debate over the preparations for 2016. A large percentage of the country's energy supply is hydro, supported by massive dams in the Amazon. Brazil is suffering from the worst drought in four decades. Rationing has begun in some of the major urban centers and the government may have to spend billions of dollars to subsidize fossil fuels to make up for the lost hydroelectric power as they did in 2014 for the Cup.

Social tensions are rising. They began in 2013–2014 in preparation for the Cup but have become more acute in the preparations for the Olympics. Since the games will be concentrated in Rio de Janeiro, the construction sites have impacted on the homes of the poor who live in *favelas* or shanty towns on the hills surrounding the city. One activist group has estimated that as many as 8,000 families have been, or are at risk of being removed from their homes. It is also alleged that many of the facilities being built in the Olympic Village will be turned over to developers and private construction companies who will build luxury housing facilities on the site.

In preparation for the influx of millions of tourists, the government has announced that they will hire an additional 2,500 medical staff in the state of Rio de Janeiro for the Olympics. The public health facilities in Brazil are of poor quality and have been underfunded for years. While new personnel are welcome, it is not clear that the needed medical infrastructure—vaccines, operating facilities, supplies, etc.—will be available.

Many Brazilians and outside observers see Brazil's having bid for two major sports events in two years as a reach too far. It represents the *grandeza* (greatness) theme that was such an important part of the Lula Government (2003–2010) when the global commodity boom and a benign international financial environment allowed Brazil to believe it indeed could achieve greatness. But the government forgot that global success rests on domestic development—education, public health, security, and adequate transportation. It also requires a competitive and productive economy, neither of which President Lula was able to achieve.

After the World Cup and the Olympics, Brazilian authorities will need to go back to the drawing board to consider what went wrong and why and what needs to be done to finally prepare Brazil for true greatness.

8

PUBLIC POLICY CHALLENGES FOR THE 21ST CENTURY

What explains the agricultural revolution in Brazil over the last few decades?

The question is often asked, "Can Brazil become competitive globally?"[1] While there are many obstacles to overcome to reach international competitiveness, there is universal recognition that the country is a global player in agriculture:

> Brazil is now recognized as the sole agricultural power in the tropics. Brazil's share in world agricultural markets (8 percent) is only second to that of the United States (17 percent) and some analysts already suggest that Brazil's share will be similar to that of the US in the next ten to fifteen years. The OECD (Organization for Economic Cooperation) and the FAO (U. N. Food and Agriculture Organization) ... projected that Brazilian agricultural production will increase 38 percent from 2010 to 2019. This huge increase in agricultural production is nearly twice the global average and several times higher than the figures prospected for giants in world agriculture such as the United States, Canada, and the European Union.[2]

How is it possible that Brazil lags in competitiveness in industrial output but stands with the traditional giants in agricultural production and exports? The simple answer is Embrapa—the Brazilian Agricultural Research Corporation, the research component of the Ministry of Agriculture, Livestock, and Food Supply, created in 1973 during the military government. It became apparent in the 1970s that the country was urbanizing very quickly and food security was an issue. It was also clear that a modern agribusiness export industry would earn needed foreign exchange to allow the purchase abroad of the inputs required for the new industrial model put in place after 1964. It was also understood in Brasília that the opportunities for agricultural expansion in traditional areas were limited. The obvious choice for new lands was the huge Cerrado in the center of the country—a biome covering about 22 percent of the country's surface area. The challenge was that the Cerrado had been seen as unproductive, and suitable only for subsistence farming. That was the first challenge for the new institution.

Critical to the success of Embrapa was the decision to organize the research unit as a public corporation; that gave the entity organizational flexibility and removed it from the heavily bureaucratic world of Brasília. The leadership was then free to recruit its own personnel, manage its budget, and to establish a personnel evaluation system. A report of the World Bank on the agency said that the success of Embrapa in transforming the Cerrado was due to adequate levels of public funding for research and development (R&D); sustained investment in human capital—currently three-fourths of Embrapa's 2,000 researchers hold a PhD; international collaboration and research excellence working with leading international universities and institutions; and a mission. The decision was made to follow an open innovation, diffusion of new cultivars (mew seeds with improved performance due to better adaptation to specific climate and soil conditions), and the filing of international patents.

The innovative approach to the Cerrado proved to be nothing less than revolutionary. Embrapa researchers decided that to focus on productivity, rather than incorporating new territory for farming, they would "lime" the acidic soil to transform it into arable land. Millions of tons of lime were poured onto the soil to reduce acidity. They also innovated in crossbreeding techniques that resulted in the development of soybean varieties that flourished in the acidic soils and that had a life cycle up to twelve weeks shorter than that of the typical plant; that allowed for two harvests a year. Another important breakthrough was the development of cotton seeds that were adapted to the semihumid tropical conditions and that produced much higher yields per hectare. The emphasis was always on developing new technologies that could be transferred quickly and easily to the farmers of the region. It was a hands-on approach that favored practice not theory.

The organization operates in all twenty-six states and the Federal District in Brazil. It has thirty-eight research centers, three service centers, and thirteen central divisions. This widespread presence allows for close collaboration between the agency and the farmers. The founders of the institution envisioned it as a broad network of research entities, each specializing in a particular topic, with decentralized control over decision making. Since its founding, "Embrapa has developed and transferred more than 9,000 technologies to Brazilian farmers. Researchers working at Embrapa have created over 350 cultivars and obtained more than 200 international patents. It is currently considered the world's leading tropical research institute."[3]

As its success was clearly demonstrated at home, Embrapa proceeded to establish bilateral agreements—research partnerships and technology transfers—with fifty-six countries and eighty-nine institutions. The organization has become a leader in south-south cooperation and conducts technology transfers with markets in Africa and the Americas. The organization also created Virtual Labs Abroad (Labex) to increase international collaboration. The United States was the first partner in the new policy. The World Bank report concludes by asking the question, "why did Embrapa succeed where other research organizations failed?"[4] The conclusion is that:

> Embrapa's mission orientation, focusing from the outset on the improvement of agricultural productivity rather than the production of scientific work, was a key driver of its success. Integration into the international flow of knowledge increased research efficiency and accelerated training. An open IPR policy—and a network of offices spread throughout the country—facilitated the dissemination of Embrapa's discoveries.[5]

Also important was sustained federal funding. Human capital development was always a high priority. And a meritocratic culture was carefully maintained and promoted. As a result of decades of results-driven research, the country is now generally ranked as the first exporter of sugar, coffee, orange juice, soybean grains, and chicken; it ranks second for beef, soybean oil, and soybean meal. For many observers, it is difficult to understand why Brazil has been able to imaginatively and successfully develop its agricultural resources while other aspects of the economy suffer from bottlenecks, low levels of investment, and related obstacles to achieving competitiveness and enhanced productivity. The challenge for the political leadership is to seriously use the creativity and innovativeness demonstrated in the agriculture sector with Emprapa in all sectors of the economy.

Is Embrapa the only success story in analyzing Brazilian competitiveness?

The other example of a success story in terms of competitiveness is Embraer, a Brazilian aerospace conglomerate that produces commercial, military, and executive aircraft. The firm is also a leader in providing aeronautical services and is today one of the country's largest exporters. Embraer has produced more than two hundred jets per year since 2008. It ranks as one of the four largest global manufacturers of civil aircraft, alongside Airbus, Boeing, and Bombardier. The company was created in 1969 (again during the military regime) as a state-owned company. It was closely related to the creation of Brazil's leading university of aerospace engineering (ITA) that developed specialized human capital; the government also promoted R&D. Embraer's proximity to ITA and its main aeronautics research and development center (CTA) ensured a steady flow of highly trained talent and created an environment that supported continuous innovation.

In its formative years, the government ensured Embraer's growth by providing production contracts for specific aircraft models and imposing import tariffs. Until 1975, the company produced for the domestic market. It survived the economic turmoil of the 1980s and was privatized by the Cardoso government in 1994. Since then, its revenue has grown at an average annual rate of 14 percent (compared to 7 percent annual growth for its main competitor, Bombardier). The firm's share of global jet exports grew from 1 percent to 8 percent in the same time period, a sign of the company's competitiveness.

Embraer is a global player today. While production remains based in São Paulo, there are offices in China, France, the United States, Portugal, and Singapore. There are two overseas subsidiaries—in the United States and in Portugal—and a joint venture with China. The government eventually removed import tariffs on aircraft components that allowed Embraer to source from global suppliers. Embraer engineers design the aircraft but turn to global suppliers for component parts in order to incorporate the best technologies at competitive prices. Since privatization, and with no further government involvement, the company has successfully pursued international contracts and has been intensely exposed to global competition and global value chains with great success.[6]

Why can't Brazil create more firms like Embrapa and Embraer?

The Getúlio Vargas Foundation's "The Brazilian Economy" recently published an edition devoted to the issue of competitiveness. In the editor's opening page, it clearly and dramatically explained what structural constraints Brazil must eliminate to attract investment and ultimately increase output growth and productivity: "infrastructure deficiencies, high labor costs, shortage of skilled workers, a high tax burden and an onerous tax system, excessive administrative burdens, shallow credit markets, as well as more direct barriers to international trade."[7]

In the same issue in an interview with Angel Gurría, the Secretary General of the OECD, he stated that the recent slowdown in global trade has exposed structural weaknesses in the supply side of Brazil's economy that went unnoticed during the commodity boom of the early and mid-2000s. Principal among these weaknesses are a fragile manufacturing sector and too little investment and savings relative to GDP. The editors point out that Brazil has been very slow in integrating into international trade and joining global value chains. In recent years, imports of raw materials and intermediate components for the manufacture of exports represent over 60 percent of global trade. A related and significant trend is the increasing share of services that now account for more than 42 percent of world trade. Brazil is far behind other countries on both measures. The consolidation of global value chains (GVCs) is leaving Brazil behind. International production, trade, and investments are increasingly organized with the so-called GVCs where the different stages of the production process are located across different countries. Globalization motivates companies to restructure their operations internationally through outsourcing and offshoring activities. Brazil has been very slow to join this dynamic and growing trend due to its limited role in global trade and the high levels of protection that make it difficult for easy import of components of the GVCs.

Gurría correctly points out that the protection that some sectors of the Brazilian economy receive discourages investment in R&D. It also inhibits training the workforce in areas that would enhance their productivity and allow domestic industry to compete globally. The geographical dispersion of suppliers has grown in recent years, facilitated by developments in telecommunications, management systems, transport, and trade liberalization. These new developments have encouraged deepening of production integration—but not in Brazil. The OECD has reported that Brazil has only 11 percent of foreign inputs in its exports. In comparison, in a much smaller economy, Chile, 18 percent of the value of mineral exports comes from imports, double that of Brazil. In another study by the Vargas Foundation, it is stated that Brazil does not import very much. The study surveyed 133 economies and Brazil is last in import-to-GDP ratio. Another study by the Foundation reported that "a successful strategy for insertion in global value chains cannot emerge from autarchic policies."[8]

A recent report by the McKinsey Global Institute (MGI), *Connecting Brazil to the World: A Path to Inclusive Growth*, supports the analysis of the Vargas Foundation and the OECD. In the Executive Summary the authors comment that:

> Brazil has become the world's seventh-largest economy, but it ranks only 95th in the world in GDP per capita. Most households have experienced only modest income growth, while inefficiencies and layers of taxes and tariffs push the prices of many consumer goods out of their reach. Having successfully lifted millions out of extreme poverty, Brazil now has to deliver on the promise of what a middle-class life really means. Productivity growth, which contributes to raising incomes and living standards, will be the key to empowering the aspiring middle class.[9]

The report also confirms that Brazilian income growth has lagged behind the global average for decades. From 1981 to

2013, the figure for Brazil was 1.1 percent; 7.7 percent for China; 4.3 percent for India; and 3.0 percent for Chile. The global average for that time period has been 1.9 percent.

The MGI report confirms the findings summarized earlier. Deeper integration into global markets and networks could provide competitive pressures that would spur Brazilian companies to innovate, invest, and modernize. For decades, national economic policy has emphasized protecting local industries and building on the strength of its vast and expanding domestic market. But this inward focus has come at a great cost to international competitiveness.

Between 2000 and 2011, Brazil's overall investment rate averaged 18 percent of GDP, well below that of other developing economies—Chile 23 percent, Mexico 25 percent, India 31 percent, and China 42 percent. And a strong currency—the flip side of success in exporting commodities—has made manufactured goods less competitive overseas, further discouraging needed investment. Productivity gains are the key to broad-based income growth that can result in wider prosperity. But the country's productivity has been almost stagnant since 2000.

The MGI agenda for Brazil includes the following:

- *Lower the cost of doing business in Brazil.* The 2014 World Bank's Doing Business Index ranks Brazil 116th out of 189 countries in terms of its regulatory burden. In the taxation category, it ranks 159th globally.
- *Continue to reduce the informal sector.* Firms operating in the informal sector can relatively easily ignore quality and safety regulations or avoid paying taxes. It represents a continuing drag on productivity.
- *Expand infrastructure.* This is a constant refrain in all studies of Brazilian competitiveness and productivity. The country's investment in overall infrastructure has fallen from 5.4 percent of GDP in the 1970s to only 2.1 percent in the 2000s. Transportation infrastructure as a share of

GDP has fallen from around 2 percent in the 1970s to less than 0.5 percent in the 2000s. Only 14 percent of Brazil's roads are paved. The railway system is inadequate. And the country's port facilities are woefully antique.

- *Build human capital.* This is the second most cited reason for low productivity and competitiveness after physical infrastructure. Brazil ranked 57th in the OECD's international student assessment 2012 report. It tested 15-year olds in 65 countries worldwide. Only half of Brazilian students would enter high school actually graduate. Brazil's needs to focus on quality; it needs to expand vocational training.[10]

The agenda for increasing Brazil's productivity and competitiveness is clear—and it has been so for many years. The political class appears stuck in time. They fail to understand the dwindling opportunities globally as other developing countries forge ahead. To fail to address the agenda in the next government (2015–2019) could have serious social and political tensions with unforeseen consequences.

Why have Chile and Mexico gotten it right?

Both countries have steadily moved to integrate their economies with global markets.[11] Mexico started to open its economy to foreign trade and investment in the 1980s. The country has thirteen bilateral and multilateral treaties with forty-five countries that allow it to trade under favored tariff terms. NAFTA was approved in 1994—with the United States and Canada. In 2014, Mexico joined the newly former Pacific Alliance with Chile, Peru, and Colombia (with Costa Rica and Panama poised to join). Trade (imports and exports together) is used as a share of GDP has grown from 39 percent in 1990 to 65 percent in 2011. China ranks 58 percent and India 56 percent; Brazil lags far behind at 27 percent. But Mexico continues to protect some sectors of the economy with tariff barriers to imports. Non-tariff barriers—rigorous customs procedures and anti-dumping laws—are in place. While Mexico needs continued attention to liberalization, it is on the way.

Chile prides itself on openness. It has signed more free trade agreements than any other nation. The 2002 Chile–US Free Trade Agreement was the first agreement between the United States and a South American country. The World Economic Forum (WEF) ranks Chile's trade infrastructure above all other countries in the region—and even the United States. Chile ranks second globally in terms of market access, behind only Singapore. Chile has successfully used its position in international trade networks to modernize its economy and follow the standards of the more advanced and competitive markets. Brazil, sadly, has not.

While Brazil need not follow the exact model of Mexico and Chile, there are clearly signs of innovation and smart policy initiatives that Brasília should consider adopting. Time is of the essence. Globalization is a reality. No country can afford to take a position of "wait and see."

Brazil's favelas—the growth of an urban challenge

With the abolition of slavery in 1888 and the collapse of the empire in 1889, Brazil's population of color was basically abandoned. Many left the plantations that had been their only home and began to move south to the developing urban areas of Brazil. Rio de Janeiro was a prime target for the newly freed Afro-Brazilians. Unable to afford housing and subject to prejudice and disdain, they settled on the unpopulated and inhospitable hills. The first favelas or urban slums had appeared in the late 19th century and were built by soldiers who had fought in the Triple Alliance War of the 1860s or the regional armed conflicts of the first years of the Republic. Released from military service, they had nowhere to live. Some of the first settlements were called *bairros africanos* (African neighborhoods) since many of the settlers were people of color.

As southern Brazil urbanized in the early 20th century, the city became a magnet for the poor in search of employment. Following the change in government that brought Getúlio Vargas to power, the early industrialization process created menial employment opportunities. These positions were filled by the new migrants. Under the Vargas government, in 1937, the Building Code of Rio de Janeiro first recognized the favelas' official existence. A housing crisis in the early 1940s exacerbated social tensions in Rio and the government began to look for ways to incorporate this new urban phenomenon into Brazilian society.

As urbanization and industrialization in the 1950s accelerated, the de facto recognition of the favela became a reality. The government talked about a public housing project but it never came to fruition. The Roman Catholic Church attempted to address the crisis but it appeared to be too little too late. But an important development hindered the growth of any coherent policy response to the slums. The federal government formally moved inland to the new capital in 1960. With the onset of the military government in 1964, the final steps were taken to consolidate the Brazilian public sector in Brasília. The slum inhabitants, by and large, did not accompany the move. A new generation of poor people from the interior, drawn to the construction opportunities in the building of the new capital, created a new generation of urban slums or favelas on the periphery of the new city.

In Rio de Janeiro, the change was a disaster. Tens of thousands of service jobs were suddenly lost and there were few alternatives. A second phenomenon boded poorly for the favelados (favela inhabitants). The military government decided to remove the favelas from their location on the hills overlooking Rio de Janeiro to peripheral areas of the state of Rio de Janeiro. The program, disguised as a government housing effort, provided no infrastructure or municipal services. The program failed because many of the favela dwellers refused to move and those that did found they did not have the means to support the cost of living in government housing.

At the end of the military dictatorship in 1980, a new challenge arose—drugs. With the US-supported program in Colombia and elsewhere, the "war on drugs" sought alternative routes for the shipment of cocaine and other substances. The Rio favelas became a convenient hiding place for the drug traffickers particularly because the Brazilian state—the police—was absent. In one favela after another, local elected leaders were forced out and replaced by agents of the dominant drug gangs. The increasingly lucrative drug and arms trade led to violent turf wars between gangs punctuated by intermittent police raids that used brutal tactics against the drug forces as well as local residents. At the same time, off-duty policemen and security agents took control of other favelas and imposed another form of violent control.

While there is mobility for favelados it is hit-or-miss. Opportunities for advancement are available but it takes a special combination of motivation, talent, and luck to succeed. That is a daily challenge for people in the slums. Few are successful, the majority are not.

The underlying reality is that the favela phenomenon is the result of decades of neglect, marginalization, and violence. The inhabitants of the favelas believe that they have been marginalized by society—and they have been. Given the erratic nature of Brazilian politics and the economic uncertainties of the last century, it has been extremely difficult to create a coherent development program for the favelas. The favelas are either demonized or romanticized. There is now favela tourism in Rio de Janeiro but that is a 21st-century effort to hide or obscure the realities of life in the slums. It will not solve the basic issues that have festered for decades.

The rule of law versus the rule of gangs

Over Brazil's recent history crime has been an extensive and ever-present public policy challenge. Throughout Brazil's daily life crime is pervasive in violent and nonviolent ways.

Over the last three decades homicide rates per 100,000 habitants have consistently been over twenty deaths a year. To put this number is context; this would make the probability of being killed in Brazil five times more likely than that of the United States.[12] The victims of violence are mainly young males between fifteen and twenty-four living in favelas or low-income regions. In 2012, 92 percent of the homicide victims were males.

Since 1998, Brazil's national crime rates have been relatively stable. Nevertheless, there have been significant changes across regions and within cities. For example, in Amazonia the murder rate rose 63 percent from 1998 to 2009. In the same direction, the murder rate in northeastern states increased almost 74 percent in the same period.

In contrast, São Paulo has successfully slashed murder rates by 62 percent over that same period. The strategy of "zero tolerance" carried out by the Social Democrat (PSDB) regional governments increased police enforcement capacities throughout the spectrum of criminal offenses and achieved a significant reduction in criminal activity. Nevertheless, the Workers' Party has criticized this policy by arguing that these policies are overwhelmingly punitive for low-income citizens and by explaining violence as a socioeconomic issue. Paradoxically, many of the regions with increasing violence have witnessed high economic growth simultaneously. For example, Amazonia increased by 50 percent its share of the GDP between 1998 and 2008.

Evidence over the last two decades points to the conclusion that crime is better explained by state capacity than by regional socioeconomic structures. However, since security is a state function and not a federal one, the fight against crime in Brazil depends on policy and electoral outcomes all over the country. As a matter of fact, the issue of crime is usually absent in presidential races.[13]

One of the historical moments where crime rose to the national and global scene was in 2006 when a criminal rebellion in São Paulo took over the city for a couple of days. On May 12, the criminal organization Primeiro Comando da Capital (PCC) ordered massive and systematic attacks against the military police in retaliation for the transfer of their leadership to high-security confinement. At the end of the second day of the riots, 299 attacks on public infrastructure were registered and thirty-eight officers and guards had been killed. The criminal syndicate's casualties totaled seventy-nine deaths while twenty-one civilians also lost their lives. Although President Lula at the time offered federal assistance, the regional government managed to subdue the rebellion through a counteroffensive and, more importantly, by negotiating with the criminal leadership to expand their prison benefits to include individual televisions and conjugal visits.

The chaotic situation expanded to neighboring states of Paraná, Mato Grosso do Sul, Minas Gerais, and Bahia through the general state of lawlessness. Subsequent investigations pointed out that much of the looting and rioting was done by civilians not related to the PCC who took advantage of the suspension of the rule of law. The São Paulo state governor at the time, Cláudio Lembo, was harshly criticized for his poor communicational and security management of the crisis.

By the end of the administration of President Lula (2003–2010), the drug lords were acting with impunity, threatening to shut down commerce in the city center, attacking municipal buildings, and killing at will. It was clear that the local police and the federal authorities were outgunned and outmaneuvered.

In the case of Rio de Janeiro the power of the drug traffickers was met with an uncommon type of policing. With the sole purpose of creating the civilian firepower to break into the most dangerous favelas, the city created the Special Operations Brigade (BOPE for its acronym in Portuguese), a polemic unit of officers trained more like special forces and less like regular policemen. The brigade operates in armored vehicles, uses weaponry that is otherwise limited to the armed forces, and its men are skilled in urban antiguerrilla tactics. The BOPE has attracted both positive and negative attention; it has inspired Brazilian action movies while at the same time being harshly criticized by international human rights watchdogs for its involvement in extrajudicial executions and civilian collateral damage. A 2005 investigation by the New York University School of Law reported that BOPE members had unlawfully killed four teenagers, claiming that they resisted arrest, after which the brigade officers falsified the crime scene to frame the victims as gang members.

Beyond BOPE's human rights record, the strategy of assaulting criminal groups has proved insufficient, since these special forces proved capable of rooting out the gangsters but incapable of establishing peace in the reclaimed favelas.

The successful bid for the World Cup (2014) and the Olympics (2016) suddenly required a new set of policies. For this reason, the Rio de Janeiro government created in 2010 the "Units of Pacifying Police" (UPP), groups of freshly recruited community policemen that establish themselves after criminal organizations have been rooted out. The stated goal was for the state to take back control of the territory from the narcotraffickers. The concept of the UPP was zero tolerance for carrying firearms. Instead of aiming to stop drug trafficking, this community police force aims to establish long-term relationships with favela residents and to give them access to public services such as health care and leisure activities for youths who are likely to work for criminal gangs.

The first operation began with a surprise attack by the Special Forces but it ended badly—scores of innocent favelados were killed in the shootout. The program then gave warning that the Units were moving into the favela—leaving time for the narcos to leave and avoid direct confrontation with the police.

Police units then set up barracks and began patrolling the communities. It was an experiment that went wrong quickly. Many of the officers in the Units were new recruits with little training or experience. The favelados often suspected them of collaborating with gangs in the confiscation and resale of arms and drugs. It was reported that the favelados had more confidence in the dealers than in the police. The human and social services—"Social UPP"—that were promised never arrived: planned job training, computer labs, improved schools and family clinics, sports and leisure facilities, and a whole array of other services were supposed to show the concern of the state for the welfare of the favela residents. Due to disinterest, bureaucratic incompetence, or corruption, the services were rarely implemented.

In preparation for the World Cub and the Olympics, the UPP expanded rapidly, but the earlier mistakes were repeated. Misunderstandings between the UPP forces and the local inhabitants did not decrease. Violence continued to permeate the "occupation." Federal troops were required from time to time to restore a semblance of order. Frequent interviews in the Brazilian press with residents of some of the largest favelas—Rocinha, Complexo do Alemão, Complexo da Mare—and scores of other favelas reported continued violence and abuse by the UPPs.

What is often overlooked in discussion of the favela phenomenon is that there is a favela culture. Music and art flourish. Slowly, over the decades, legally or illegally, the slums have obtained access to water and electricity. A number of nongovernmental organizations (NGOs) are active in providing social assistance, medical care, and basic education. Given the apparent inability of any level of government—municipal, state, or federal—to find a comprehensive solution, the status quo will continue indefinitely. Although there is evidence that drug smuggling and violence has been reduced in the enclaves controlled by the UPP, some of the criminal leadership has moved to other parts of Rio de Janeiro which will make future conquest increasingly difficult.

The UPP phenomenon demonstrates another reality in 21st-century Brazil. The police forces are poorly trained and poorly paid. They often see financial opportunity in participating in the arms and drug trading that are part of daily life in the favelas. There is also a social stigma since the favelados are generally of darker complexion than the UPP forces. Racism is present in all aspects of Brazlian society and the favelas are no exception.

Despite the multiple options for policing styles of the regional governments, there is a key role that the federal government can play in reducing violence. Because of Brazil's historic development of a national military-industrial complex, criminals do not need to import their weapons. In fact the NGO Viva Río has estimated that 76 percent of all illegal guns seized by security forces are produced domestically.[14] For this reason, regulating domestic production can go a long way in curbing violence.

Are gender issues in Brazil receiving enough attention?

The historical reality for women in Brazil is that the country began as, and has remained for many centuries, a patriarchal society. Men were the "father figure" in the home, identified in the literature of the time as authoritative and strong; women were weak and subservient. It was unheard of for women—other than as day laborers on the plantations or farms—to work outside the home. Equality has come very slowly for women in Brazil. They did not receive the vote until 1932, and it was only in the 1960s that they were given adult rights—previously they had to receive permission from their husbands or fathers to leave the country or open a bank account.

The issue is complicated in Brazil because of the large number of Afro-Brazilian women. Disparity in opportunity and income levels exists across racial lines, with black women often having fewer options to allow them to work outside the home. While the country has reduced inequality and poverty over the last decade, women's wages are 84 percent of that of their male counterparts. Moreover, the gender wage gap increases with higher education: women with twelve or more years of education earned only 58 percent of men's salaries. Additionally, women carry most of the work related to family chores (even when working full time): Women devote an average 25.1 weekly hours to caring for their families while males devoted only ten hours per week for the same purpose.[15]

Since the restoration of democracy in 1985, women's status has been evolving positively. The progressive participation of women in formal jobs, the expansion of women's education, and a greater role in family leadership has changed their place in society. New public policies and agencies have been created and included in the government agenda to foster gender equality. During the decades of the 1980s the Conselho Nacional dos Direitos da Mulher (National Council of Women's Rights); the Conselhos Estaduais da Condicão Feminina (Regional Agencies of the Condition of Women); and the Delegacia Especializada de Atendimento a Mulher (Specialized Police Station for Women) were created.

In 2004 the "Plano Nacional de Politicas para Mulheres" (National Plan of Policies for Women) was established to combat gender discrimination and to consolidate educational policies from an equal gender perspective. In the same year, "Plano Nacional para Saude da Mulher" (The National Plan for Women's Health) aimed to guarantee women's sexual and reproductive rights. In 2006 a law against domestic violence, the "Maria da Penha" Law, was passed, and has led to the arrest and conviction of a large number of men on charges of abuse. The law tripled the severity of sentences for offenders. Under the law regarding violence against women, any action or omission based on gender that causes death, injury, physical, sexual, or psychological suffering or harm is a basis for criminal proceedings. The law has proven to be very effective, particularly for poorer women.

There has been a great deal of thought about women who reside outside the large cities in Brazil. Programs such as "Minha Casa, Minha Vida," (My house, my life), created in 2009, help people with low incomes to buy their own house;

it is estimated that 80 percent of the beneficiaries are women. The "Bolsa Familia" (Family Packet) program, created in 2003, through which payments are transferred by the federal government to poor families in the name of the woman of the family, are helping to consolidate the role of women in society.

The Brazilian government is committed to meeting the obligations of United Nations and other programs aimed at eliminating discrimination against women. And the fact that the current president of Brazil is a woman and that in the 2014 national election, there were two women candidates—President Rousseff and Senator Marina Silva—indicates that the once all-male club of Brazilian politics is dissolving. Progress has been made in terms of guaranteeing women's rights in Brazil, but old attitudes disappear slowly. Implementation of the existing laws remains a challenge, especially in rural areas. Justice in Brazil is not always blind, as is the case in many countries, with regard to the rights of women. But the trajectory is positive. A younger generation of women have become aggressive advocates for gender equality and it is difficult to imagine that they will be deterred from continuing to expand the frontiers of equality in Brazil in the 21st century.

Will Brazil continue to pursue a successful strategy to deal with HIV and AIDS?

In his memoir, President Fernando Henrique Cardoso comments that:

> If there was another cause where it didn't hurt to have a sociologist running Brazil, it was with regard to AIDS. By 1990, Brazil faced a catastrophe. We had the same rate of HIV infection as South Africa, at just over one percent of the adult population. Our infection rate was the highest in Latin America and our health care system, long neglected by the military regime, was unable to cope.[16]

Cardoso went on to state that the question was whether it was better to deny the existence of the problem or deal with it. At that point in history, governments were generally unwilling to confront issues such as homosexuality, prostitution, and other sexual matters, and hoped AIDS would go away. The challenge for Cardoso was that "sex was just not something that elected officials talked about" (p. 214).[17]

The president nicely stated the reality in Brazil about sex. While the Brazilian people, generally, had an open attitude about sex, more so than in many other countries, it was not the custom for the government to become involved in discussing sexual preferences. Indeed, public opinion appeared to support a liberal approach to individual choice, but expected a more sober and conservative posture on the part of the government. The Cardoso government (1995–2003) decided to address the AIDS epidemic openly. Millions of condoms were distributed during Carnival each year. With the help of NGOs, the government staged informal events in poor neighborhoods to educate people about the problem. The AIDS threat was publicized across the country with large billboards and blunt TV ads. Students received comprehensive sex education classes that emphasized the importance of honesty in relationships.

As part of the campaign to address the AIDS threat, the government passed a law in 1996 guaranteeing Brazilians free access to antiretroviral AIDS drugs. The government understood that to offer universal coverage, the cost of treatment had to be considerably reduced. At the time the antiretroviral medicine was prohibitively expensive for poor countries. The government began to encourage Brazilian pharmaceutical companies to produce cheaper, generic versions of foreign AIDS medicines that were not protected under local patents. And the authorities lobbied foreign firms with patent protection to cut their costs for the Brazilian market. If they refused to do so, the government threatened to break the patent and produce them in Brazil.

This created an international crisis. The foreign companies asserted that lower prices would prevent them from producing new drugs. The US government presented a complaint before the World Trade Organization (WTO), arguing that Brazil's position was in violation of international property right laws. Over the next few years Brazil conducted an international campaign to build a coalition of allies. In June 2001, as a United Nations AIDS conference was scheduled to open in New York, the United States withdrew the complaint against Brazil from the WTO. Global public opinion was a critical component of Brazil's victory.

As a result of the Cardoso government's campaign, today the HIV and AIDS epidemic in Brazil is classified as stable at the national level, with a prevalence rate in the general population of 0.4 percent. Over the last two decades, policies have been developed to deal with those groups that are most vulnerable—prisoners, sex workers, gay men and women, transgender people, and drug users. The Brazilian Department of STD/AIDS and Viral Hepatitis (DDAHV) has been decentralizing its HIV testing services throughout the country. Strategies have been implemented in partnership with NGOs to scale up testing among key populations.

While the program, overall, has been successful, obstacles remain. The Catholic Church and many evangelical communities are opposed to the use of condoms. Younger Brazilians who are too young to remember the epidemic at its worst are often careless and have adopted an "it can't happen to me" attitude. Further research must be done on new antiviral drugs. Testing needs to be expanded especially in the poorer sections of the country. The medical authorities recognize the ongoing challenges. They are working to raise awareness and to provide universal care, but budget cuts and competing priorities will be a challenge in the 21st century in the ongoing fight against the spread of HIV/AIDS.

Brazil's indigenous people

The 1988 Constitution recognized indigenous peoples' rights to pursue their traditional ways of life and to the permanent and exclusive possession of their "traditional lands," which are demarcated as Indigenous Territories. But the constitutional protection has been largely ignored. An indigenous rights organization, Coordination of Indigenous Organizations of the Brazilian Amazon (COIAB), has tried but failed in its efforts to call attention to the plight of the native population. During the government of President Lula (2003–2010), major dam projects were begun such as Belo Monte, mentioned earlier. FUNAI, underfunded and often ignored, confronted powerful political forces in Congress that supported the illegal occupation of indigenous land. The profits were enormous and the indigenous organizations too weak to threaten or veto continued incursions. In the last two decades, there has been a boom in the exploitation of the rainforest for mining, logging, and cattle ranching. The encroachment continually degrades the rivers and soil of the native people.

The fate of the native population in Brazil is intricately tied to the deforestation of the Amazon rainforest and to the aggressive and often illegal abuse of Indian indigenous lands. While there are many voices in civil society and in the international community who are concerned about the fate of the native population, it is, ultimately, a sovereign issue for the Brazilian government to decide the future of its territories. For many in power in Brasília, the native population issue has little relevance when compared to the larger policy challenges the government faces. It remains to be seen whether the universal campaign for indigenous rights will impact public policy in time to save the dwindling community of native Brazilians.

Deforestation and the future of the Amazon Basin

Brazil has always been at the center of any discussion of greenhouse gases; it is the seventh-biggest emitter in the world. Emissions from the country's energy sector continue to grow, and have increased by 44 percent in the past decade. Brazil is home to a large part of the Amazon rainforest, and 35 percent of the country's emissions are a result of ongoing deforestation.

But in response to both domestic concerns and international pressure, Brazil, over the past decade, has reduced its emissions from the land sector by about 85 percent. This is the largest decline in greenhouse gas emissions of any country in the world.

In recent years, the domestic impact of climate change has become more evident with the increase of extreme weather events. Many Brazilian communities remain highly vulnerable to the impact of these events, due to issues such as poverty and poor urban planning. Flooding has become a reality in many towns and cities. The Brazilian government has been an active participant in global climate negotiations. At meetings in Kyoto, Japan (1997); Copenhagen (2009); and other conferences, and most recently in Paris (December 2015), at the COP21 conference, Brazil has argued for a durable legally binding climate accord. As the Paris conference opened, Brazil joined the so-called "high-ambition coalition" group advocating for a durable deal with a strong review every five years. The United Nations climate summit in Paris was a meeting of the Kyoto Protocol parties and sought to replace the Kyoto Protocol, which called on the developed countries to cut the emission of greenhouse gases.

The Paris meeting was the 21st Conference of the Parties to the United Nations Framework Convention on Climate Change (UNFCCC) created in Rio de Janeiro at the 1992 Rio Earth Summit, at which countries recognized the need to limit global warming. The Rio Summit began a long and continuing dialogue regarding greenhouse gases and emissions. From a reluctant participant, Brazil has become an active partner in the process and has indicated that it must be at the center of any comprehensive agreement given the presence of a large part of the Amazon basin as part of its national territory. It now remains to be seen whether or not the COP21/Paris agreement will actually be implemented and whether or not Brazil will be able to manage the political pressures to ignore measures to limit emissions in the Amazon.

For centuries following the discovery of Brazil the Amazon rainforest was a relatively underpopulated, remote, and somewhat mysterious part of Brazil. The rubber boom at the end of the 19th century brought some attention to the region but it was for a very short period of time. The first national focus came under the presidency of Getúlio Vargas in the 1940s, but World War II and Vargas's fall from power in 1945 precluded any policy development. With his reelection in 1951, Vargas established the Superintendency for the Economic Valorization of Amazonia (SPVEA) in 1953. But his suicide in 1954 downgraded the region in national planning. After the military assumed power in 1964, a number of institutional initiatives were taken. In 1966, the Superintendency for the Development of Amazonia (SUDAM) was created, and in 1970, the National Institute for Colonization and Agrarian Reform (INCRA) was established. These new organizations paralleled a number of developments in the military regime.

While Amazonia was not well developed, it had become a geopolitical concern for the armed forces. Given the resources of the region, would other countries, at some point in time, attempt to encroach on the Basin? The geopolitics led the military to initiate a massive road-building program to integrate the region with the rest of the country. The Transamazon Highway aimed to provide access to settlers who would strengthen the national presence. And commercial interests became increasingly interested in the Amazon. Cattle ranching was one of the first major contributors to deforestation. Brazil is the single largest beef exporter in the world, exporting about two million tons of beef per year. Massive amounts of the forest were destroyed to make way for the herds of cattle. With new technologies, soybean cultivation became profitable. Small subsistence farmers, attracted by the availability of land, "slashed and burned" their way through the jungle. Logging became profitable, contributing to the loss of thousands of acres of trees. And as we have seen, massive hydroelectric power projects were begun to furnish electricity for the large urban centers in the south of the country. The dams not only added to the deforestation issue but had severe negative implications for the indigenous peoples living in the region. (As mentioned earlier, Marina Silva, the two-time presidential candidate and former Minister of the Environment in President Lula's government, resigned over the aggressive dam construction agenda of the government. Her Green Party has become a major player in national politics).

Powerful political interests emerged around these activities and were successful in lobbying the federal government to overlook legal restrictions on deforestation. The "ruralist" lobby was successful in 2012 in having Congress reform the Forest Protection Law to give amnesty to those who chopped down more than their allocated limit prior to 2008, and made massive reductions in how property needs to stay forested in various areas where the state zoning permits cultivation. A combination of power politics; poor law enforcement (IBAMA, the federal environmental enforcement agency, responsible for land regularization, only collects 1 percent of the fines it imposes); ambiguity about land titles (it is estimated that of the privately owned land in the Amazon, only 14 percent is actually backed by secure land deeds); and corruption have made it difficult to control deforestation.

But beginning in the mid-1990s, in response to the growth of a green movement in Brazil, and international pressure to stop the deforestation process, the federal government began to actually implement legislation on the books. The Brazilian Forest Code stated that, on every farm in the Amazon, 80 percent of the land had to be set aside as a forest reserve. This had been overlooked or ignored for decades. Bans and restrictions became the policies of choice by the federal government to enforce the Code. Beginning around 2005, in his first term in office, President Lula made deforestation a priority. That resulted in better cooperation between different agencies of the government, especially the police and the public prosecutors. It is estimated that the area in which farming was banned was increased from a sixth to nearly half the forest.

Parallel to the new enforcement measures, new technologies allowed ranchers to raise more animals on less land. There was also the beginning of a consumer boycott against products grown or produced in illegal farms or ranches. After a campaign by Greenpeace (an environmental lobby) and others, buyers of Brazilian soybeans promised not to purchase crops planted on land cleared after July 2006.

The final policy initiative dealt with the expansion of soybean cultivation. Farmers in the thirty-six counties with the worst deforestation rates were banned from receiving cheap credit until those rates fell. The government also created a proper land registry, requiring land owners to report their properties' boundaries to environmental regulators. There was a cattle boycott modeled on the soya one. And for the first time, there were rewards as well as punishments: an amnesty for illegal clearances before 2008 and money from a special $1 billion Amazon Fund financed by foreign contributions for compensation payments.

As of 2016, deforestation in the Amazon rainforest, while not halted, has slowed. While there are fluctuations year by year, the trend is positive. And increasingly a concern over "green space" has become popular at municipal and state levels. The city of Curitiba, in the southern state of Paraná, has been termed the greenest city on earth. A combination of astute municipal leadership and a set of policies that reduced pollution—a rapid transit system that reduces carbon emissions by 25 percent by reducing the use of automobiles and a program that exchanges trash and recyclables for bus tokens, food, and cash—has demonstrated that eco-savvy urban planners can make a difference.

The challenge for the Brazilian government is to remain vigilant in the implementation of existing rules and to find the political courage to resist political pressures from loggers, farmers, cattle ranchers, and soybean cultivators to embrace and protect the initiatives defined at COP21. More emphasis needs to be given to local and state programs such as that in Curitiba. Brazilians, with the right incentives, are as sensitive to pollution and carbon emissions as any other people on the globe.

9

FOREIGN AFFAIRS

Why are diplomatic relations between the United States and Brazil so unpredictable?

Although Brazil is a large country, it is not a powerful country. The asymmetries between the United States and Brazil are an important irritant in the bilateral relationship. For more than a century, the United States has been recognized as the most powerful nation-state—economically and geopolitically. While that may be open to interpretation in the 21st century, in most global arenas the voice of the United States predominates.

That is not true of Brazil. While the country has increased its regional presence through trade and diplomatic agreements, it has failed it its efforts to secure a permanent seat on the Security Council of the United Nations. Brazil has sought the support of the United States to do so but the government has been reluctant to provide the endorsement needed. There is resentment in Brazil that the United States has openly endorsed India for a position on the Council—another important emerging market player. With the exception of Brazil's important contribution to the Allied cause in World War II, Washington has not considered Brazil a reliable partner. There is little interest in Brasília in becoming involved in any of the conflicts in the Middle East. In the Western Hemisphere, Brazil has tacitly supported countries that are in diplomatic conflict with the United States—Venezuela and Bolivia, for example. The bilateral relations have been tense and often misunderstood since the end of World War II in 1945.[1]

The United States was strongly—and publicly—in favor of democratization in Brazil as the War appeared to be ending. Washington welcomed the overthrow of Getúlio Vargas and seemed to believe that the armed forces were apolitical and had facilitated the transition to a civilian regime. President Harry Truman visited Brazil in September 1947 and endorsed the democratic government. The conservative Dutra regime regularly supported US Cold War policies. But the relationship began to deteriorate when it became clear that Rio de Janeiro expected extensive financial support from Washington. It was difficult for Brazil to understand that the rebuilding of Europe through the Marshall Plan, the reconstruction of Japan, and the containment of China after the communist victory of 1949 preoccupied the Truman administration. Washington appears not to have understood the depth of Brazil's sense of rejection, given the strong relationship during the War. The Truman White House advocated foreign direct investment as the most appropriate path to economic development in the Hemisphere. This was not viewed sympathetically in Rio de Janeiro. Once again, a sense of neglect and frustration characterized the relationship.

While Brazil felt left out of US concerns, the government in Rio de Janeiro remained supportive of US foreign policy goals after 1945. Reflecting the growing antagonism between Washington and Moscow, the government severed diplomatic ties with Russia in 1947 and, in the same year, closed the Brazilian Communist Party (PCB). In 1949, the US armed forces, at the request of the Brazilian high command, were instrumental in establishing the Superior War College (ESG), using the US National War College as a model. ESG became a conservative think tank for civilians and military officers. It would be the backbone of the government that followed the overthrow of the Goulart government in 1964.

In response to a growing concern that it was important to remain on Brazil's good side, and in spite of the disappointment over financial assistance, President Truman created a

Joint Brazil–United States Technical Commission in 1948. Its task was to identify necessary policy reforms to increase the country's competitiveness. The outcome was probably predictable—an emphasis on foreign direct investment.

It became clear by the end of the Truman administration in 1952 that the strong ties of the 1940s did not provide a basis for strong ties in the 1950s. While Washington remained committed to a solid relationship with Brazil for Cold War reasons—opposition to communism—the two nations were pursuing different priorities. The one issue that did elicit mutual agreement was the increasingly aggressive regime in Buenos Aires, that of Juan D. Perón. His attempt to find a "third way" in global affairs was a matter of concern to the White House. And the traditional antipathy, even hostility, between the two South American nations was a matter of mutual interest to Washington and Rio de Janeiro.

In hopes of winning public support from the Dutra government for the War in Korea, the United States granted Brazil a $25 million loan from the Export-Import Bank to build the country's first steel mill at Volta Redonda in 1950. To further ensure Brazil's support, or at least neutrality, in Cold War affairs such as Korea, the United States created another joint Economic Commission in 1950. Unlike its predecessor the new Commission supported the creation of the Brazilian National Economic Development Bank (BNDE) that, as we have seen, became a major factor in supporting the government's development goals for decades to come.

Did the return of Getúlio Vargas to power in 1951 contribute to a deterioration of US–Brazil relations?

The Vargas that returned to the presidential palace in 1951 was an older and perhaps less savvy individual. He seemed to blame the United States for his overthrow in 1945. While Getúlio supported the Korean War diplomatically, no troops were committed. His support was based on Washington granting Brazil increased financing for infrastructure projects. The Brazilian Congress actually voted against sending troops to Korea, but Brazil did recognize the Republic of Korea in 1949.

From Washington's viewpoint, Getúlio became more erratic and more nationalistic in the early 1950s. He created a state oil monopoly, Petrobras, in 1953 and called it a symbol of Brazil's independence from the United States. He issued a decree limiting profit remittances by foreign companies operating in Brazil. And as Washington provided financial aid for countries like Mexico and Argentina, Brazil felt slighted even though the amount that Brazil received after 1945 was about the same granted to other countries in the hemisphere.

Things changed little with the arrival of Dwight Eisenhower in the White House in 1953. Cold War–focused and conservative, the new US administration emphasized foreign direct investment over grants or concessionary loans. The opinion in Washington by the end of 1953 was that Brazil was incompetent in economic affairs. Getúlio Vargas's left-leaning domestic and foreign policies did little to endear him to the White House. But as the Cold War deepened, voices in the administration urged caution in US dealings with Brazil. Dr. Milton Eisenhower, the president's brother and advisor on Latin American affairs, visited Brazil in July 1953, just after the second joint economic commission had been closed. Dr. Eisenhower remained a strong supporter of close relations between the two countries. But as President Vargas became overwhelmed by the crosscurrents in domestic civilian and military politics, relations were basically on hold.

Why did relations not improve with the election of President Kubitschek?

With the suicide of Getúlio Vargas in 1954, observers hoped a new phase in the bilateral relationship might be feasible. The election of Juscelino Kubitschek (JK) in 1955 appeared to support that optimism. JK enthusiastically supported foreign direct investment. His suggestion to create a hemisphere-wide development strategy—Operation Pan-America (OPA)—was viewed in Washington as an interesting concept and it complemented Washington's growing concern over communist influence in the Americas. That concern deepened after January 1, 1959 and the collapse of the Batista regime in Havana.

Secretary of State John Foster Dulles visited Brazil in August 1958 and reiterated Washington's hope for a continued strong relationship with its neighbor. President Eisenhower traveled to Brazil in February 1960 in hope of winning the country's support for the United States' growing concern over the Castro regime but Brazil remained uncommitted—unless it received a promise of financial development assistance—which it did not. Official Washington continued to insist that ties with Brazil were a significant part of American foreign policy in the hemisphere. But that position did not result in development assistance in any significant amount. The Eisenhower White House welcomed President-Elect Jânio Quadros to Washington but the short-lived administration left Washington confused and uncertain of the next steps to be taken. Jânio appeared determined to pursue an independent foreign policy. Washington asked the president to support Washington's anti-Castro policy, especially the Bay of Pigs invasion; he declined to do so. In spite of his unpredictability, the United States extended $100 million in new credits in May 1961 but that did not change the atmosphere between the two countries. His sudden resignation on August 25, 1961 and the succession of Vice President João Goulart in September 1961 would open a new chapter in the bilateral relationship.

Was 1961 the beginning of the end of the post-1945 relationship with Brazil?

President Quadros's inauguration coincided with that of President John F. Kennedy in 1961. The Kennedy White House announced the Alliance for Progress within weeks of the new government taking office. The White House was keenly aware of the growing distemper in Latin America and hoped that the Alliance would provide a new opportunity to work closely with its neighbors in the hemisphere. In an eventful meeting in Uruguay in August 1961 the charter for the new initiative was signed, and only Cuba chose not to do so. The Alliance was indeed a new beginning in the bilateral relationship given that it provided, for the first time since 1945, substantial development assistance. Quadros was noncommittal on the Alliance. But the White House's concern over developments in Brazil increased dramatically with the arrival of João Goulart. His reputation had preceded him as a favorite of the nationalist left. But it was determined in Washington that the continuation of the Cold War required caution and patience with the untried Brazilian government. In an effort to establish a working relationship, President Goulart visited the United States in April 1962. He addressed a joint session of Congress. The White House announced the Northeast Agreement, a significant financial package to be administered by the US Agency for International Development (USAID) and the Brazilian Superintendency for the Northeast, located in Recife, Pernambuco.

But Brazilian politics, as we have discussed, radicalized quickly and dramatically in 1962–1963. The US embassy in Rio de Janeiro, led by Ambassador Lincoln Gordon, became increasingly concerned over the drift to the left by Goulart and his supporters. The White House was alarmed over what it perceived to be communist penetration in Brazilian politics and society. President Kennedy sent his brother, Attorney General Robert Kennedy, to Brasília in December 1962, to warn Goulart over the dismay in Washington over the country's radicalization. Goulart was apparently noncommittal but assured the Attorney General that any threat from communism could be easily controlled. With the economy in tatters, Kennedy stated that there would be no further economic support unless the government took steps to introduce reasonable economic measures to control inflation.

As we have discussed, May 1964 was the end of the "experiment with democracy" in Brazil. Lyndon B. Johnson had succeeded to the presidency in November 1963 after the assassination of Kennedy. There was heightened concern in Washington that Goulart was deliberately going to establish a communist state. While the White House did not plan the coup d'état of March 1964, it welcomed it publicly. The United States moved quickly to recognize the acting president, as Goulart fled into exile.

The year 1961 was, with hindsight, the end of the post-1945 bilateral relationship. It was impossible to work with the quirky Jânio Quadros. João Goulart, weak and indecisive, could not—or would not—attempt to create a democratic center in Brazilian political life. The close linkages between the two military establishments would provide the basis for the transition from failed democracy to the creation of the first "bureaucratic-authoritarian" state in the region as the military decided it was time for a regime change. Initially, the United States welcomed the new, firmly anticommunist government. But that welcome would soon wear thin.

Was the arrival of the Castelo Branco administration a plus for US–Brazil relations?

The relationship between Brasília and Washington changed dramatically with the arrival of the military in power. President Castelo Branco's government became a strong and dependable partner of US foreign policy. Relations with Cuba were broken. Brazil committed troops as part of an Inter-American Peace Force that was sent to the Dominican Republic in 1965; a Brazilian general was the commander of the Force. Brasília endorsed US goals in Vietnam. A significant amount of development assistance materialized from the US government and the multilateral institutions in Washington, DC. It seemed that the "unwritten alliance" was back in place. But to the dismay of official Washington, the regime was soon viewed as authoritarian, in spite of the "democratic" credentials of President Castelo Branco. There appeared to be a sense in the White House that the traditional role of the Brazilian military would reassert itself—intervene, reorganize, and exit. This, of course, was a serious misreading of the deeply felt belief in the armed forces that they had saved Brazil from "going communist" in the nick of time. They were determined to guarantee that the threat of communism would be eliminated before any talk of a democratic transition.

There is still an historical debate as to whether or not a more critical position by Washington in 1964 might have convinced the military to begin a rapid transition to democracy. I believe, as I have stated, that the military was in no mood to take advice or admonishment from anyone, including the United States. It would be a long twenty-one-year period before the United States would be able to see a return to democracy in Brazil.

Why did succeeding military governments downgrade relations with the United States?

The second government of the 1964 "Revolution" took office as the Brazilian "miracle" was about to begin. It was also a government of the "hardliners" in the Brazilian armed forces. These two realities set the stage for a distancing of Brasília from Washington. The Brazilian government believed it was in a position to pursue a more independent foreign policy, one not automatically linked to the United States. Brazil was about to enter its *grandeza* (greatness) phase of development. The government had no desire to be drawn into the long and ultimately tragic US involvement in Vietnam. Costa e Silva's government supported the peaceful development of nuclear technology for developmental purposes. Ambassador Lincoln Gordon was recalled to Washington and his replacement knew little about Brazil and became increasingly skeptical of the regime. The third military government, that of General Emílio Garrastazu Médici, talked about reestablishing democracy but did little to actually implement it. It became clear that his government had no interest in joining the United States in its war against communism.

The US personnel presence was scaled back. By the late 1960s, it was clear in Washington that there would be no democratic transition anytime soon. Indeed as the regime consolidated, and became more visibly repressive, members of Congress, religious groups, students, and journalists began to demand that the United States recognize the realities in Brasília. Economic aid to Brazil began to be questioned as well. But it soon became clear that Brazil had easy access to international capital markets and to financing from the multilateral institutions in Washington, DC, and was far less reliant than in 1964 on financial support from the US government.

The Nixon administration did not see why it should give priority to Brazil if that country did not support American foreign policy goals. But on one important issue, Médici was different than his predecessor. He did want to eradicate leftist regimes in the Americas; in that, he and Richard Nixon were soulmates. Médici visited Washington, DC in December 1971 and apparently the two chief executives "bonded" over their mutual disdain for governments they viewed as aligned with the communist elements in their societies. While there was a good deal of talk about restoring the positive relationship, it basically remained at the rhetorical level. There was little agreement on trade matters, with Brazil seeking trade concessions that were politically unfeasible in Washington. The administration of President Gerald Ford took no new initiatives and relations remained cool and proper.

It was clear by the mid-1970s that Brazil no longer saw itself in a tutelary relationship with the United States. Economically, although not true, Brasília believed it had turned a corner in its deepening of industrialization, its program of domestic infrastructure development, diversification of trade, and access to global capital markets. While anticommunism was a theme that brought the countries together it was insufficient to create the circumstances for a strategic partnership.

Did the Carter administration deliberately set out to antagonize Brazil?

Two important events occurred to shape the bilateral relationship. The first was the arrival in Brasília of the fourth military government, that of General Ernesto Geisel in 1974—the return to power of the Castelo wing of the armed forces. The second was the unexpected success of Governor Jimmy Carter's presidential campaign and his election in 1976. The Carter White House inherited a festering foreign policy dilemma: nuclear power. After the first oil shock in 1973, Brazilian policymakers reviewed their options. At the time, Brazil imported about 80 percent of its petroleum. To guarantee continued economic growth, nuclear power seemed a reasonable policy choice. Brazil negotiated a contract with Westinghouse to purchase two nuclear reactors. But the US government, feeling the impact of the increase in oil prices, decided to suspend new contracts for new supplies of enriched uranium that forced Westinghouse to cancel the contract.

Brazil, determined to guarantee energy supplies, turned to West Germany and concluded an agreement that provided for the delivery of up to eight nuclear power plants in exchange for uranium exports to Germany. The United States was dismayed by Brazil's decision. Did this mean that Brazil had decided to "go nuclear" and did that imply the country would produce energy not only for peaceful purposes but to become a nuclear power? The situation was even more complicated because Brazil had refused to sign the Nuclear Nonproliferation Treaty (NPT), alleging that to do so would relegate the country to second-class status among the larger nation-states. It was pointed out at the time that Brazil had also refused to sign the 1969 Treaty of Tlatelolco that sought to establish a nuclear-free zone in the region. From the viewpoint of Brasília, Washington was once again attempting to dampen the *grandeza* of Brazil. The Brazilian armed forces were particularly sensitive to this sort of perceived offense.

The White House sent Vice President Walter Mondale to Germany in an attempt to convince Germany to cancel or postpone the deal. The government refused. Mondale's trip was viewed in Brazil as yet another attempt to limit Brazil's global reach. Deputy Secretary of State Warren Christopher visited Brasília in an effort to explain the Carter administration's position but to no avail. Furious with the US bullying, the Brazilian government cancelled the 1942 military cooperation agreements between the two countries.

The second issue that poisoned relations during the Carter administration was that of human rights. Following the disastrous end of the Vietnam War, the US Congress came under pressure to include respect for universal human rights in the goals of US foreign policy. Legislation was passed in 1973 and again in 1975. The latter required that the Department of State report annually to Congress on the state of human rights in any country that received US military assistance. And at the end of the administration of President Gerald Ford, Congress required the administration to cease any aid to any nations that were considered to be violators of basic human rights. The first report was issued by the State Department at the beginning of the Carter administration in early 1977. Human rights, of course, had been a major part of the Carter campaign and dominated his inaugural address.

Brazil was infuriated, since the report singled out the Geisel government for deliberate violations of human rights. Brasília refused to accept any further military assistance; there would be no further US oversight of what the military believed was a completely internal matter. It became very clear to the Geisel government, rightly or wrongly, that Washington did not understand the depth of the guerrilla threat to Brazilian political stability. But the human rights policy did receive support from many parts of civil society in Brazil as the authoritarian state became increasingly repressive, to the dismay of the regime.

US–Brazil relations were further damaged by a number of initiatives taken by Brazil as part of its increasingly aggressive independent foreign policy. Brasília recognized the Marxist government in Angola in a direct rejection of Washington's position. As trade with the Middle East increased, the Brazilian Foreign Ministry, Itamaraty, was viewed as anti-Israel, a key ally of the United States. Suddenly the Carter administration realized that a line had been crossed and it was necessary to step back and attempt to restore some level of dialogue with Brasília. Secretary of State Cyrus Vance visited Brazil as did President and Mrs. Carter, and a series of other high-level officials. But the fifth military government of General João Figueiredo (1979–1985) retained, defiantly, the country's independent foreign policy. Much lip service was paid to the importance of Brazil, but as usual, more immediate challenges—Cuba and the civil wars in Central America—occupied much of the day-to-day time of US policymakers. Brazil was not necessarily ignored, but it was not a priority.

Could succeeding administrations have reset the alliance?

While nuclear issues continued to be important to the White House, the advent of Ronald Reagan (1981–1989) saw a new source of concern for Brazilian policymakers. Brazil and much of Latin America was entering the "lost decade" of debt and possible default. The second Middle East war in 1979 sent oil prices skyrocketing. It became increasingly difficult for most of the countries in the region to service their global debt obligations. When Mexico defaulted in August 1982, international lenders refused to provide any more credit to the region but debt obligations were expected to be met. Brazil led the charge to find a political solution to the issue of insolvency. The Reagan administration did support bridge loans for Brazil but both President Reagan and Prime Minister Margaret Thatcher of the United Kingdom insisted that the developing economies recognize and meet their international debt obligations. For many observers the real motivation of the two leaders was to protect the private commercial banks that had been the principal lenders to the Third World. The crisis would not end until 1989 when the administration of President George H. W. Bush devised a scheme to reduce the debt burden. There were trade skirmishes over computers, differences of opinion on a series of issues at the United Nations, and no interest in endorsing the Contra wars in Central America. Brazil reestablished diplomatic relations with Cuba.

The administrations of the first President Bush and that of President Bill Clinton found it difficult to establish anything more than cordial relations with the now democratic Brazil. President José Sarney (1985–1990) and Fernando Collor de Mello (1990–1992) traveled to Washington, DC and were treated with courtesy but little else resulted from the visits. Trade disputes were the principal policy issue in the 1990s. But Clinton was unable to win fast-track negotiating authority from Congress and Brazil ultimately walked away from the 1994 Free Trade of the Americas (FTAA) initiative during the George W. Bush administration. That ended any prospects for further gains in the trade regime. President Bush visited Brazil in 1992 and President Clinton in 1997. Clinton personally organized the financial rescue package for Brazil in 1998 when the Asian crisis reached Brazil and the two presidents apparently established a personal rapport. But that did not result in any new policy direction in Washington toward Brazil.

The presidency of George W. Bush (2001–2009) began with warm words for Latin America, but the focus of the White House became consumed with other geopolitical issues following the terrorist attack of September 11, 2001. Brazil's independent foreign policy did not allow the country to play a role in either Afghanistan or Iraq. But, as was expected, President Bush praised Brazilian democracy during his visit in 2005. As the geopolitical crises of the first Bush administration became more routinized, the second administration began to reassess the US relationship with Brazil. A strategic dialogue was negotiated. But it never functioned very well. Presidents Lula and Bush met a number of times. It was only at the end of the Bush presidency that Brazil took front and center in Washington's thinking. As the financial crisis unfolded, after the collapse of Lehman Brothers in September 2008, Brazil and like-minded developing countries pressured the industrial nations to reconvene the Group of Twenty (G-20), the major world economies.

President Bush convened a G-20 Summit in Washington at the end of his administration and after the election of Barack Obama. Brazil's Minister of Finance, strongly supported by fellow BRICS, argued for an urgent set of consultations to resolve the financial crisis. At a succeeding summit (they are now held annually) in the United Kingdom in 2009, Presidents Lula and Obama apparently established a strong working relationship. But the tide turned quickly and frictions emerged. Brazil was critical of Plan Colombia, a bilateral US aid program for the Colombian government in their civil war against terrorists. Also, Brazil would not support sanctions against Iran, and President Lula, along with Prime Minister Recep Ergodan of Turkey, attempted to negotiate an agreement with Iran for a nuclear swap between Iran and Turkey in 2010. The diplomatic effort was a misconceived effort by President Lula of Brazil to play a larger role in world politics. Turkey, also interested in expanding its diplomatic weight in world affairs, agreed to join the Brazilian initiative. The United States was taken aback since its efforts to broker a deal had been underway for some years. Washington reacted negatively to the undertaking since Brazil had demonstrated little interest in the Middle East region prior to the hastily organized initiative, which failed to gain any traction. The US was not pleased and became even more displeased when Brazil and Turkey voted at the United Nations against sanctions on Iran in June 2010.

The Obama administration continued the policy of previous administrations in not recognizing Brazil's candidacy for a seat on the Security Council of the United Nations. This has been a critical goal of Brazilian foreign policy for years. Brasília was critical when Obama did acknowledge India's candidacy during his state visit to New Delhi in November 2010. The president paid a state visit to Brazil in March 2011 but the event was overshadowed by the decision of the White House, during the trip, to send troops to Libya. Brazil had abstained on the vote at the United Nations to authorize force against the Libyan regime. After a meeting with President Obama, President Rousseff commented that the relationship has been characterized by "empty rhetoric." Any deeper relationship must be between equals. She called for the United States to lower trade barriers to Brazilian exports.

Rousseff visited the United States on an official visit in April 2012. The two presidents met cordially at the White House and in general terms discussed cooperation. As one commentator stated after the visit was over, it merely reinforced the state of "benign neglect" between the two countries. Plans were made for a state visit in 2013, but it was abruptly cancelled when it was revealed that the US National Security Agency (NSA) had allegedly intercepted President Rousseff's email messages, those of her aides, and of the state oil company. The allegations were based on documents leaked by former intelligence contractor Edward Snowden and published in the British *Guardian* newspaper. The Brazilian government has demanded an apology which it never received. In hopes of rebalancing the relationship, Vice President Joe Biden traveled to Brazil in June 2014 to attend the US–Ghana soccer match as part of the World Cup. He met with President Rousseff in an effort to clarify the Snowden affair. The two nations agreed to disagree. As the Brazilian presidential campaign got underway in 2014, there was faint hope that any further bilateral initiatives would emerge until 2015, at the earliest.

Writing in the *New York Times* after a visit to Brazil in 2014, Roger Cohen stated:

> There may be more perplexing international relationships in the world than the troubled one between the United States and Brazil, but there are not many. A natural friendship has fissured under unnatural strain. A perverse estrangement prevails. Brazil, a kind of tropical United States, finds it difficult to connect in Washington, and vice versa. The nation that might have been America's closest ally (even without a formal alliance) among the rising powers is now anything but.[2]

As a result of that estrangement, Brazil made a strategic decision to buy Swedish fighter jets rather than Boeing's F/A-18 Super Hornets. At the end of 2014, plans for cooperation in defense, renewable energy, and nuclear and space technologies were in limbo until at least 2016 or longer. There is little expectation, as the Obama administration terminates in January 2017, that relations will improve in the foreseeable future. Monica Hirst has written about the relationship and the title of her book summarizes the current state of affairs—*The United States and Brazil: A Long Road of Unmet Expectations.*[3]

Does Brazil prefer regional foreign policy initiatives in lieu of a global policy?

Although Brazil has signaled its desire for an expanded role in world affairs, it appears to be most comfortable in regional initiatives. Clearly in trade matters it thinks globally. As we have discussed, the BRICS group is important. But the consistent theme in foreign affairs has been the hemisphere. Under President Cardoso, Brazil hosted the first summit of South American leaders (not Latin American leaders) in Brasília in 2000; a second summit took place in Guayaquil, Ecuador in 2002. At the third meeting in Peru in December 2004, the heads of state signed the Cuzco Declaration, a two-page document setting in motion the creation of the South American Community of Nations (SACN). The new entity brought together two preexisting subregional trade blocs, Mercosur and the Andean Community of Nations (comprising Bolivia, Colombia, Ecuador, and Peru) as well as Chile, Guyana, and Suriname. The Declaration called for the new organization to develop a common currency, a tariff-free common market, and a regional parliament. According to the Secretary General of the Andean Community at the time, the "ultimate goal, which can hopefully be reached, in time, is the United States of South America."[4]

The SACN leaders met in Brasília in September 2005 and agreed on steps to formalize their agreement. Twelve nations signed the constitutive treaty of the Union of South American Nations (UNASUR) that replaced the SACN, at a summit hosted by President Lula in Brasília in May 2008. In December 2010, Uruguay became the ninth state to ratify the UNASUR treaty, thus giving the union full legality. The treaty entered into force in March 2011. The treaty set goals for the integration of regional energy and transportation networks, immigration policy, and related topics. There were plans to create a UNASUR parliament in Cochabamba, Bolivia. A Bank of the South was a future goal to be located in Caracas, Venezuela.

The organization designates a President pro tempore each year. The first president was Michelle Bachelet of Chile; the latest is Desi Boutere of Suriname. The presidents of the organization meet annually and the foreign ministers convene every six months for planning and consultation. The headquarters is located in Quito, Ecuador. The office of Secretary General was created as well and the first to hold that office was former president Nestor Kirchner of Argentina; the most recent is the former president of Colombia, Ernesto Samper, in 2014. There are a number of ministerial councils for specific policy areas.

A South American Defense Council was created in March 2009. Its main objectives are the consolidation of South America as a zone of peace and a basis for democratic stability. The UNASUR leaders have made it clear that this is not a traditional military alliance such as NATO. Thus far, UNASUR has operated at the margins of South American diplomacy. There have been efforts to facilitate a dialogue, for example, between the socialist government of Venezuela and it domestic political opposition, but with little success. The organization has stated that if asked, it would support the peace talks in Havana, Cuba between the government of Colombia and the guerrilla organization, the FARC. While these are worthwhile initiatives, the organization has had difficulty in identifying a more robust role in the region.

Brazil took the lead in hosting the first Latin American and Caribbean Summit for Integration and Development (CALC) in a summit held in Bahia in December 2008. Plans were made at the summit to fold the Rio Group into CALC. The Rio Group (the first meeting was held in Rio de Janeiro) was created in December 1986 and grew out of regional efforts to negotiate an end to the Central American conflicts of the early 1980s and to oppose unilateral intervention by the United States in the region.

In yet another effort to support regional integration, CALC was succeeded by the Community of Latin American and Caribbean States (CELAC) according to the Declaration of Caracas, in December 2011. CELAC consists of thirty-three countries in the Americas and represents more than six hundred million people. The Caracas meeting was strongly anti-American, with the late President Hugo Chavez calling for the organization to replace the Organization of American States (OAS), which is seen by the leftist populist presidents of countries like Venezuela, Nicaragua, Bolivia, and Ecuador as a tool of American imperialism. The first meeting was held in Santiago, Chile in January 2013; the third was convened in Havana, Cuba in January 2014. The "Havana Declaration" stated that:

> The unity and integration of our region must be built gradually, with flexibility, with respect for pluralism and the sovereign right of our peoples to choose their own political and economic system . . . and reaffirm as a general principle that the strengthening of CELAC as a political forum and actor in the international arena is one of our priorities.[5]

Given that the meeting was held in Cuba, stressing "pluralism" was important to the leftist populist governments in the region and to the government of the Castro brothers. It is noteworthy that in all of these meetings over the last decade or so, neither the United States nor the European Commission have been invited to attend—even as observers. In the case of Brazil, the country's foreign policy has favored regionalism and south-south diplomacy. While Brazil was a strong voice during the financial crisis in the late 2000s, the PT favors like-minded nation-states when addressing social and political issues. While not questioning the intentions of the states of the region in pursuing greater integration, the disparities among them will continue to make it difficult. Politically, they vary from centrist democratic governments like Peru, Chile, Uruguay, and Colombia; to the more dogmatic leftist governments like Venezuela, Nicaragua, Ecuador, and Bolivia; to the left-leaning governments like Brazil. Economically, there are nation-states like Argentina and Venezuela in perpetual crisis, as well as governments like Chile, Colombia, and Uruguay that are modernizing and market-oriented.

But CELAC holds out more promise than UNASUR or other initiatives in recent years. At the Santiago summit, the heads of state instructed their foreign ministers to create a CELAC-China cooperation forum. In April 2014, Costa Rica convened the first CELAC meeting of ministers of economy and industry aimed at developing sustainable production in the Americas. In the same month, a CELAC delegation met with the Minister of Foreign Affairs of China, Wang Yi, to discuss the cooperation forum. The delegation also met with Vice President Li Yuanchao and other Chinese officials. As the forum has begun to consolidate, China has increased its presence in the region—in addition to the strong trade ties, China and Costa Rica have announced the creation of a special economic zone in the Central American country. Costa Rica is the largest trading partner of China in the region and China is Costa Rica's second largest trading partner in Central America.

While it is too early to determine whether or not CELAC will be a more dynamic actor in the hemisphere, the early signs are positive. Brazil is a strong supporter of the Community; it complements its overall emphasis on regional integration and cooperation. The Community also represents the changing contours of the hemisphere's foreign policy as Asia emerges as an attractive trade and—hopefully—investment partner. During his July 2014 visit to Brazil, President Xi Jinping met with eleven Community leaders and announced the establishment of a China-CELAC forum. The Chinese leader said that the official establishment of the new forum will be in Beijing during an inaugural ministerial meeting. The Chinese head of state indicated that the creation of the forum will be a strong signal of China's commitment to strengthening coordination with the region and promoting south-south cooperation.

Is China a positive or negative partner for Brazil?

China is now Brazil's largest trade partner, having replaced the United States in 2009. Both are active members of the BRICS. There are frequent diplomatic exchanges between the two countries. But in recent years, criticism has grown that the dependence of Brazil on China's trade patterns is disadvantageous for Brazil.[6]

The two countries had distant but cordial relations for many years before the coming of the Communist Party into power in

1949 and the creation of the People's Republic of China (PRC). Brazil continued to recognize the Republic of China, now located in Taiwan. Bilateral ties were reestablished in August 1974 when embassies were opened in Beijing and Brasília. For a moment in the 1960s China received greater attention from Brazil during the independent foreign policy of President Jânio Quadros. Vice President João Goulart was in China when Quadros resigned and Goulart returned to Brasília to assume the presidency. The military takeover in March 1964 ended any further overtures to China until the end of the Cold War. President Cardoso (1995–2003) visited China during his first term of office and President Jiang Zemin paid an informal visit to Brasília in April 2001; he had previously stopped in Brazil in 1993. His successor, Hu Jintao, visited Brazil in November 2004 as the trade relationship began to dramatically increase, and President Lula was invited to Beijing for a state visit the same year. During that visit, the two countries launched the "China-Brazil High-Level Coordination and Cooperation Committee." The Committee consists of eleven subcommittees ranging from economic cooperation to scientific and technological development.

The decade of global economic growth that began in 2002–2003 provided Brazil an historic opportunity to maximize its agribusiness success. China became a major buyer of Brazilian commodities; it also purchased large amounts of iron ore for its steel industry. In 2003, as the relationship deepened, trade totaled $6.5 billion; by 2012 it was $75 billion. In percentage terms, trade with China ballooned from 2 percent of Brazilian trade to 17 percent. China and Brazil communicated frequently during the financial crisis in 2008–2009. They were also deeply committed to south-south diplomacy. They shared a common global agenda within the context of the BRICS grouping. President Lula traveled again to China in May 2009 with a large business delegation.

President Hu Jintao was in Brazil for the second BRICS summit in April 2010 (the first had been held in Russia in 2009).

It was during this period that strains began to appear in the relationship and the issues were trade and investment. Brazil's exports to China consist of commodity and semiprocessed, commodity-based exports such as iron ore, vegetable products, crude oil, and pulp and paper. China sends to Brazil high-value-added goods such as machinery and electrical equipment, chemical products, base metals, and textiles. Brazilian businessmen complained of deindustrialization given the imbalance. And this led to a demand for protection. President Rousseff's government has moved to protect local industry with new anti-dumping regulations and tax relief. The Brazilian car industry, once highly competitive, had become increasingly worried about Chinese automobile manufacturing in Brazil. In response Rousseff's government imposed a 30-percentage-point tax increase on cars with less than 65 percent local content, taking the tax on some imported models to a punitive 55 percent on top of import tariffs. These policies have raised questions about Brazil's respect for the guidelines of the World Trade Organization (WTO). But clearly they were driven by domestic political considerations and the concerns of the automobile industry.

A year earlier, President Rousseff had made her first visit to China and the major theme of the trip was the need for China to purchase not only commodities and raw materials but higher-value-added products. In response to Brazilian pressure, Chinese and Brazilian companies signed thirteen deals and cooperative agreements that included the purchase of thirty-five E 190 planes by Chinese airlines from Brazilian aircraft manufacturer Embraer, worth about $1.4 billion. Embraer also signed an agreement with the state-owned Aviation Industry Corporation of China to manufacture the firm's Legacy 600 business jet. Brazil's national electric company Eletrobras and the state-run energy firm Petrobras also signed agreements with their Chinese counterparts.

Prime Minister Wen Jiabao met President Rousseff in June 2012, on the sidelines of the Rio+20 sustainable development summit meeting sponsored by the United Nations. Both countries stated that they now were partners in a "global strategic partnership." Both leaders agreed to a common agenda of investments in the mining, industrial, aviation, and infrastructure sectors to encourage bilateral commerce.

Attracted by the possibility of increased petroleum exports from Brazil, in October 2013, CNOOC and China National Petroleum joined forces with Royal Dutch Shell and Total to participate in the Petrobras-led consortium exploring Brazil's vast Libra oil field. In the area of financial services, China's Construction Bank Corporation agreed that same month to purchase 72 percent of Brazil's mid-size bank Banco Industrial e Comercial for $726 million. But these agreements have not slowed the complaints of deindustrialization by Brazilian business leaders.

Most recently, President Xi Jinping began his second official visit to Latin America in July 2014. His visit to Brazil was to attend the sixth BRICS summit in the northeastern city of Fortaleza. Increasingly sensitive to the discontent in Brazil over the imbalanced trade relationship, the two presidents signed agreements for the sale of another sixty Embraer passenger jets to China. There were early discussions of Chinese participation in a trans–South American railway. The two leaders also considered Chinese participation in the completion of a railway from Brazil's northeastern Atlantic coast across the Amazon Valley to Peru's Pacific Coast. The railway would help ease the severe bottlenecks Brazil has in getting its commodities, like soy and iron ore, to market efficiently. And these products are destined for China.

During the visit it was announced that the Export-Import Bank of China will provide $5 billion over three years to support Brazilian mining conglomerate CVRD to purchase or lease equipment, vessels, and other services from Chinese companies. The Bank of China has also signed a deal to help CVRD arrange global financing for the next three years. Both presidents recognized that 2014 was the fortieth anniversary of the establishment of bilateral diplomatic relations. In a joint statement, both presidents pledged to deepen their partnership and to increase communication on regional and global issues. They agreed to continue efforts to reform the multilateral organizations and to seek greater clarity in global financial procedures. A decision was taken to start the first China–Brazil comprehensive strategic dialogue at the foreign minister level.

Over the decade or so of bilateral involvement, Brazil and China have established an amicable relationship. But the obvious area of friction is the inability of Brazilian industry to increase its productivity and competitiveness, as we discussed earlier in this book. China is very dependent on Brazil for raw materials and commodities and will continue to be so for the foreseeable future. Brazil is also a valuable ally for Beijing in reforming the global agenda in favor of the developing world. There is also skepticism in both capitals about the United States and its foreign policy goals and interests. China will continue to stress the strategic partnership between the two nations. More agreements will be negotiated and signed; some of which will come to fruition, many of which will probably not. China will provide sufficient financing for Brazilian priorities for the government in Brasília to be able to confront those who argue against the growing influence of China in Brazil. But the truth is that the relationship is "stuck." The resource curse—the country's historical dependence on raw material and commodity exports to the neglect of higher-valued manufactured goods—is a reality in Brazil and will not change unless fundamental reforms are undertaken by Brasília. That possibility seems unlikely to happen in the short term.

10

BRAZILIAN CULTURE AND SOCIETY

Brazil has a vibrant national culture. It ranges from the passionate commitment of the average Brazilian to "their" soccer team to the bossa nova, an imaginative film industry, and Carnival. These colorful and fascinating aspects of life in Brazil are as important as government changes, political personalities, and the ups-and-downs of the São Paulo stock market. They demonstrate the enthusiasm of the *povo* (people) of Brazil for enjoyment, creativity, and if you are a *carioca* (a resident of the city of Rio de Janeiro), living in a *cidade maravilhosa* (the most marvelous city . . . in the world).

But it is also a society dealing with important questions of gender diversity, acceptance of alternative lifestyles, and a forceful response to the AIDS epidemic, when most of the world wanted to ignore it or hoped it would go away. But it all starts with *o Jogo Bonito.*

Brazil and O Jogo Bonito *(The Beautiful Game)*

Soccer is deeply ingrained in Brazilian popular culture: ask any adolescent or teenager of any class to identify Pelé—who led the team to victory in 1958, 1962, and 1970—Garrincha, Kaká, Cafu, or Romario and you will receive a highly emotional recitation of the great superstars of the game over the last few decades. The Brazilian national football team has won the FIFA (International Federation Football Association) World Cup tournament a record five times: in 1958, 1962, and 1970 (the year in which Brazil was awarded the Cup permanently); 1994 (led by the legendary 3 "R's": Ronaldo, Rivaldo, and Ronaldinho); and 2002 (when Brazil, in a brilliant final, defeated Germany). It is the only team to succeed in qualifying for every World Cup competition ever held. It is advisable not to mention the 1950 final game, played in Brazil, when the team lost at the last minute to Uruguay (known universally now as the *Maracanazo*—the Maracanã blow—named after the stadium in Rio de Janeiro where the game was held) or 2014, when Germany played an impressive game (to win their fourth title) to defeat the Brazilian team at Maracanã that appeared to have forgotten how to play.

The British brought soccer to Brazil in the late 19th century. It was played initially in private clubs, dominated by European immigrants. The national team played it first game in 1914. The team's first appearance in the World Cup was in 1930. By that decade soccer had moved on to the streets and beaches of Brazil. The game is a great social equalizer. Mixed racial teams will have a pick-up game on the beach on weekends or in improvised neighborhood fields. Players are all known by their nicknames or first names (as are many politicians in Brazil—Lula and Dilma for example). The word "Pelé" for the country's superhero has no particular meaning, but no one knows the player by his formal name—Edson Arantes.

The year 2014 was not auspicious for the World Cup and Brazil. The team had lost in 2006 and 2010 due to poor coaching, in the eyes of the public, and the absence of superstars. Moreover, the country was in a nasty mood. The Game has always cost a great deal of money. Billions were committed by the government of President Lula (who touted Brazil's winning the competition to host the game in 2007 as Brazil's coming out moment). But a large portion of the commitment was in public-private partnerships, meaning that the tax revenues of the Brazilian people would help fund the effort. The government committed to building or repairing twelve stadiums, some in small cities deep in the interior of the country; many questions were raised as to their utility after the games were over.

By 2013–2014, it was clear that the economic growth of the previous decade had ended. Questions were raised as to whether or not the country could afford the Game since there appeared to be little money for improving education and public health and local transportation. Constant media coverage reported how slow the construction process was and raised the question of whether or not the country would be embarrassed if the original plan fell short. The country's mood was not helped by the emerging scandal in FIFA over allegations of bribes, fraud, money laundering, and rigged bids to host the Cup.

The national team's performance in 2014 was lackluster at best. A great debate began after the team's defeat as to the future management of the game. But there is no indication that Brazilians are going to abandon their passionate commitment to "the beautiful game." Needed leadership changes will take place in preparation for the 2018 game (hosted by Russia). New stars have appeared—such as Neymar—around whom the next national team can be built. Brazil and soccer are intertwined and no separation is viewed as possible by the Brazilian public.

Culture—High and low

If *o jogo bonito* is the national passion for Brazilians, music must be a very close second. Brazilian and US music have a long history dating back to the mid-19th century. As one of Brazil's most famous composers has said,

> the only music that really swings is that of the United States, Brazil, and Cuba, all places where the black thing and the white thing mixed. The rest, with due respect to the Austrians, is all waltzes.[1]

One important "import" to Brazil was Luis Moreau Gottschalk, who moved to Rio de Janeiro in the mid-19th century. A Louisiana native, he quickly became a well-known professor for a new generation of Brazilian musicians. At the beginning of the 20th century, musicians and composers began talking about "cultural cannibalism." The implication was clear—Brazilian musicians and composers looked abroad for new ideas, integrated them into the current musical trends, and made them Brazilian. It is said that an ensemble of young musicians recorded what was probably the first samba. Their music traveled to Europe and the group embarked for Paris and became part of the 1920s rage for "new" and modern music—out with the old, in with the new.

Brazilian music took the United States by storm in the 1930s with the emergence of the legendary Carmen Miranda. An important movie star in the heyday of Hollywood, she performed Brazilian music in night clubs, on stage, and on film. The next stage of the evolution of Brazilian music was "bossa nova" that became popular at first in the bars and clubs of Copacabana and Ipanema in Rio de Janeiro.

Bossa nova

One of the most famous of Brazilian music genres is the ever popular bossa nova. The exact origin of the term "bossa nova" is uncertain. Within the artistic beach culture of the late 1950s in Rio de Janeiro the term "bossa" referred to any new "trend" or "fashionable wave." In early-20th-century poetry, the word "bossa" was slang for something was done with particular charm, a natural flair, or innate inability. Bossa nova has at its core a rhythm based on samba. But is not to be confused with American jazz. Overall, as one commentator said, the rhythm has a "swaying" feel rather than the "swinging" feel of jazz. Bossa nova is usually played on the nylon string classical guitar, with the fingers rather than with a pick. The lyrical themes are true to life in Brazil—love, women, longing, homesickness, nature, and the best of youth. Bossa nova prior to the military takeover in 1964 was more "bourgeois."

After the coup, it became more confrontational, referring explicitly to politics, repression, and liberty. The names most identified with bossa nova are João Gilberto, Antônio Carlos Jobim, Chico Buarque, Gal Costa, Sérgio Mendes, Vinicius de Moraes, Elis Regina, and Caetano Veloso—and many more. If the Beatles were to Europe and the United States the new musicians in town, the bossa nova generation took Brazil—and the world—by storm. The "Girl from Ipanema" captures the beauty and the allure of bossa nova.

Samba

Bossa nova has at its core a rhythm based on samba but samba is among the most popular music genres in Brazil and is generally thought of as the country's national musical style. Think samba and think Carmen Miranda and Carnival. It developed from a mixture of European and African music, with its roots in West Africa. It was brought by slaves to Brazil in the colonial period and originated in the northeast state of Bahia. Modern samba emerged in the early 20th century and was first popularized in Rio de Janeiro. Samba uses a distinct set of instruments, all of which produce an instantly recognizable sound.

Brazil has produced a number of other musical genres—*choro*, MPB, *frevo, forro, maracatu, sertanejo, brega,* and *axe.* All are related, in one way or the other, to slavery, early colonial experiences, experimentation, and improvisation.

During the military dictatorship (1964–1985), a new musical form emerged in part in response to the Beatles and to rock'n'roll—"Tropicalismo"—a revolutionary new style. Seen as "unrevolutionary" by the military and their conservative supporters, key figures like Gilberto Gil and Caetano Veloso were jailed. Following their release, they went into exile in London and began to absorb the work of Pink Floyd and Led Zeppelin, among others. When they returned from exile, they continued to experiment, and today "Tropicalia" is the background for the music scene in the 21st century.

Carnival

Considered the largest street carnival in the world, the Rio de Janeiro Carnival attracts thousands of foreign visitors every year. While many cities around the world celebrate pre-Lenten carnival, Rio apparently does it best. In large part the festival is linked to the well-organized and financed Samba Schools. These are large social entities with thousands of members and a special theme for their song and parade each year. The parade of the Samba Schools is a spectacle, if seen, never to be forgotten. Hundreds of thousands of dollars are spent on costumes, floats, musicians, and support staff. Carnival takes place in the six weeks directly before Easter in the Christian world. It is the final set of events before the somber tones of Lent begin. Masks are worn to hide identities, costumes can be serious or frivolous, and at the heart of life each day and night is the pulsating beat of the samba bands.

Film

The first cinema in Brazil opened in Rio de Janeiro in 1897, started by an Italian immigrant. The industry was not taken seriously for a number of decades except for the musical comedies and short dramas that starred Carmen Miranda. Brazilian cinema came of age in the 1950s, more or less at the time of the emergence of bossa nova. Rio de Janeiro in the years leading up to the military coup in March 1964 was experimental city.

The first significant film was the famous *Black Orpheus* (*Orfeu Negro*) that was shot in the Morro da Babilonia favela in the Leme neighborhood of Rio. It was released in 1959 and directed by a Frenchman, Marcel Camus. The film is based on the play *Orfeo da Conceição* by Vinicius de Moraes, one of the stars of the Bossa Nova. It is a Brazilian adaptation of the Greek legend of Orpheus and Eurydice, set in the modern context of a favela in Rio at carnival time. The film is particularly famous for its soundtrack by two Brazilian composers, Antônio Carlos Jobim and Luiz Bonfa; the two songs became bossa nova classics. The film ends in tragedy, as the legend tells us, but in the 20th century it won the Palme d'Oro at the 1959 Cannes Film Festival, the 1960 Academy Award for Best Foreign Language Film, the 1960 Golden Globe Award for best Foreign Film and the BAFTA (UK) award for the same category. *Black Orpheus* opened a short, golden age of Brazilian cinema; a revival only took place after the end of the dictatorship and the restructuring of the Brazilian economy beginning in 1994.

Since then, there have been a number of Brazilian films with an international following and often with a strong social message. In 1998, *Central do Brasil* (Central Station) was nominated for two Oscars and won another forty-one awards. It focused on the emotional journey of a former schoolteacher who helps a young boy search for his father after his mother had passed away. The film is shot in Rio de Janeiro and the Brazilian northeast. *Cidade de Deus* (City of God) was released in 2002. It follows the lives of two boys growing up in a favela. One becomes a drug dealer, the other a photographer. It is a violent film that pits one young generation of children involved in drug-running against another. The final scene shows the latest survivor group deciding to write a list of the next group to be eliminated. One boy turns to the group and asks, "but does anyone know how to read and write?" The film captures daily life in the favelas of Rio and the terrible deficit in basic education in modern Brazil.

11

CONCLUSION

SOME FINAL REFLECTIONS

Was the 2014 presidential election totally unpredictable?

As the Brazilian election cycle began in the spring of 2014—with the first round of voting on October 5—the general expectation was that the PT would nominate incumbent President Dilma Rousseff and that she would win, perhaps outright in the first round, but certainly in the second round of voting (October 26). Former President Lula would be a strong supporter and the loyal lower class created by Bolsa Família would carry the day. But analysts began to point out that the Achilles heel in this scenario was the economy.

The rating agency Standard & Poor's had recently cut the country's sovereign debt rating to the lowest investment-grade rating, citing weak macroeconomic indicators and increasing debt, as well as constrained policy options in an election year. In 2008, when Brazil achieved investment-grade status, Brazil's potential GDP was estimated at around 4 percent; in mid-2014, estimates were around 2 percent. Inflation in 2008 was viewed as stable at around 4 percent; long term expectations in mid-2014 were around 6 percent. The current account deficit, in the same time period, increased from 2 percent to 4 percent. Other analyses were as pessimistic, pointing out that the microeconomic reform agenda was stalled. There was no serious discussion in Brasília about tax reform, accelerated infrastructure investment, or a technological upgrade to increase productivity.

It was also becoming obvious that public discontent was rising over the cost overruns and failures in the planning for the World Cup in the summer months (winter in Brazil). As one commentator reported:

> Brazil plowed billions of dollars into building a railroad across arid backlands, only for the long-delayed project to fall prey to metal scavengers. Curvaceous new public buildings designed by the famed architect Oscar Niemeyer were abandoned right after being constructed. There was even an ill-fated U.F.O museum built with federal funds. Its skeletal remains now sit like a lost ship among the weeds. . . . Some economists say the troubled projects reveal a crippling bureaucracy, irresponsible allocation of resources, and bastions of corruption.[1]

The article quotes one watchdog group that analyzes public budgets: "We're waking up to the reality that immense resources have been wasted on extravagant projects when our public schools are still a mess and raw sewage is still in our streets."[2]

Other analysts placed the economic slump in a broader social context. Santiago Levy of the Inter-American Development Bank pointed out the following:

> The creation of Latin America's new middle class has generated a revolution of expectations. But countries' ability to continue delivering on these expectations may not be there. It is a whole new political game . . . it is low productivity growth that could make the middle class vulnerable. You cannot have sustained rises in real wages without sustained increases in productivity.[3]

As President Rousseff's standing in the polls dropped from 55 percent to 48 percent at the end of April, her opponents began to look more attractive. As expected, the lead opposition candidate was Senator Aécio Neves, from a long-standing traditional political clan from the state of Minas Gerais. He was the nominee of the PSDB, the party of former President Cardoso. His grandfather had been the heir apparent in March 1985 at the time of the transition to democratic government, but took ill and died shortly thereafter. Neves had been a successful congressman from his home state and an impressive governor as well. He chose a respected political leader from the state of São Paulo as his vice-presidential candidate, recreating the old *"café com leite"* coalition of times past. He was viewed as "market-friendly" and in favor of much-needed structural reforms.

The surprise of the campaign was the decision of Governor Eduardo Campos of the northeastern state of Pernambuco to declare his candidacy. He too came from a well-known political family in the state. His grandfather, Miguel Arraes, had been governor of the state when the military coup took place. He was exiled but returned after 1985 to run successfully again for the governorship. Eduardo Campos had served as his grandfather's cabinet chief. He had served as a federal congressman and briefly as Minister of Science and Technology in President Lula's government. He represented the Brazilian Socialist Party (PSB) and was serving as the party president when he announced his candidacy. It was assumed that Campos was positioning himself for 2018 since he was not well known outside the northeast region.

It was noted that Campos had welcomed Marina Silva into the PSB after the Supreme Electoral Court blocked the foundation of her own party. Silva had also served in the Lula administration as Minister of Environment but resigned after disputes within the government over the Belo Monte project and related policy differences. She had also served as a federal senator and had garnered almost 20 percent of the national vote in the 2012 elections. She was from a poor family of rubber-tappers in the Amazon and was a self-made political leader. In a surprise development, Campos asked her to serve as his vice-presidential candidate and, after some hesitation, she decided to accept.

By July 2014, the race became more interesting in that there was reporting that indicated the race would go to a second round and that it was possible for Aécio Neves to defeat the incumbent president. In the middle of August, the totally unexpected happened. Eduardo Campos was killed in a plane crash in São Paulo. A leader of the next generation was gone. The PSB deliberated whether or not to replace Campos with Marina Silva and decided to do so. She, in turn, chose a federal deputy from the southern state of Rio Grande do Sul, Beto Albuquerque, as her running mate. He had close ties to the agribusiness sector long suspicious of Silva because of her environmentalist record. The opinion polls immediately confirmed that Marina Silva was surpassing Aécio Neves and closing on President Rousseff. Suddenly the election was about change. Was Silva that agent? In one respected poll, 70 percent of Brazilians said that they want the next government to change everything or almost everything in the way Brazil was governed.

In late August it was announced that the country had been in recession in the first half of the year as investment dropped. The economy took an even bigger downturn in the second quarter, contracting 0.6 percent from the first quarter. The government statistics bureau, IBGE, also revised down its estimate for first quarter activity to 0.2 percent contraction, meaning the economy had entered a recession. This was the first recession since the global financial crisis of 2008–2009. The government blamed the poor showing on global economic weakness but opponents replied with charges of mismanagement.

In the first television debate of the campaign, in late August, Silva appeared to finish first, calling for a "new politics." In early September a national poll, for the first time, gave Silva a ten-point lead over President Rousseff in a second round. As her campaign surged, it released a 242-page "government plan." The major points included a pledge to bring inflation back to the center of the target of 4.5 percent; to generate a primary surplus; to work with a free-floating exchange rate with no intervention from the Central Bank; and to create an independent "Fiscal Responsibility Council" that would verify and assess the execution of the budget as well as develop analysis for long-term budget planning. These were all viewed as mainstream, centrist proposals—and seen as market-friendly. It was noted that Silva had assembled a set of economic advisors that was viewed as professional and competent.

Questions began to be raised about Silva's capacity to govern, if elected. It was pointed out that the October 5 election was not only for president and vice president but for twenty-seven governorships, all 513 seats in the Federal Chamber of Deputies, and one-third of the eighty-one Federal Senate seats. There were some twenty-five political parties in the running, and to govern successfully the winner would need to bargain and negotiate to put together a majority coalition. The PT began to insinuate that Silva, relatively inexperienced, would be unable to do so. President Rousseff's supporters also observed that her strong "green" stance would alienate the farm lobby, a powerful political force in Brazilian politics. Silva stated, in the course of the campaign, that increasing agricultural output and protecting the environment are not contradictory goals and that she favored sustainable development of the country's vast farming potential.

Will Brazil confront the issue of race relations in the foreseeable future?

As discussed earlier in this volume, Brazil was the last country to abolish slavery in 1888. Of the estimated 10.7 million African slaves shipped across the Atlantic between the 16th and 19th centuries, approximately 4.9 million were destined for Brazil. *The Economist* recently reported:

> The pervasiveness of slavery, the lateness of its abolition, and the fact that nothing was done to turn former slaves into citizens all combined to have a profound impact on Brazilian society. They are reasons for the extreme socioeconomic inequality that still scars the country today.[4]

A number of studies have confirmed that Afro-Brazilians generally are to be found in the poorest regions of the country and will have lower levels of education and are less likely to be upwardly mobile. In the urban areas, the higher the income of the population, the higher is the contingent of the white population. The less the income, the higher the black and *pardos* population (mixed race). The same happens in the rural areas, the lower the income, the higher proportion of blacks and *pardos*.[5]

The World Bank estimates that people of African descent constitute about 45 percent of the country's population. They earn half the average income of the white population. Prejudice and racial discrimination are key factors in the exclusionary process that characterizes Brazilian society: 62 percent of the poor live in households headed by nonwhites.[6]

In general, the elite in Brazil tend to be white. This includes the judiciary, Congress, and industry. Women of color rarely achieve prominence in public life. An exception is Marina Silva who has been a presidential candidate twice, a federal minister, and a member of Congress. The Workers Party has prided itself on the advances it has made in addressing race and class in Brazil. One important policy decision was the introduction of racial admissions quotas in more than seventy public universities. In Rio de Janeiro's state universities, 20 percent of places are set aside for black students who can pass the challenging entrance examination. Another 25 percent are reserved for a "social quota" of pupils from state public schools whose parents' income is less than twice the minimum age—and who are usually black. The federal government has also begun a program to award grants to black and *pardo* students at private universities.[7] These initiatives have been controversial. Critics argue that quotas are another form of racism. Others maintain that quotas undermine equality of opportunity and meritocracy. But it would appear that, at least in the area of higher education, there is finally a commitment to supporting the integration of blacks and *pardos* in 21st-century Brazil. But as Zezé Motta, Brazil's leading black actress and a longtime campaigner for black advancement, commented in an article in *The New York Times*, "we have gone from the hold of the ship to the basements of society."[8] Clearly, there remains a great deal to be done to move the society toward fuller equality.

There are many reasons why Brazil needs to address the continuing marginalization of its population of color. They are excluded from most executive positions in the private sector. Social mobility in Brazil is clearly linked to the color of your skin. Without equal opportunity in school, the black and *pardo* population remains "stuck" in poverty. In politics, the black and *pardo* population are clearly underrepresented. The challenge for Brazil is to seriously address this centuries-old social issue with clear and transparent policies to open opportunities and advancement for a significant part of the population.

A final word

The continued revamping of the institutional structures of the region has created some confusion and has raised questions about the long-term priorities and even the survivability of organizations like UNASUR and CELAC. Are they in competition? Do they overlap? Is another version in the making? All of that remains to be clarified. Whatever transpires in the future, Brazil will be front and center in working with its neighbors.

In September 2014 the polls continued to indicate that Silva was gaining on Rousseff and had replaced Neves in second place. But by late September, the polls turned. A "fear" campaign, launched by the President's supporters, appeared to be successful and the results of the first-round of the election on October 5 confirmed that it had been. President Rousseff carried 41 percent of the vote, Neves 33 percent, and Silva a disappointing 21 percent. The surprise was the strong showing of Neves and the fall from grace of Silva. As the competition for the final round of voting on October 26 began, the question was whether or not Marina Silva would endorse Aécio Neves and whether her supporters would turn out on Election Day in his favor.

Brazilian stocks soared on the Monday after the election. Neves was seen as pro-business; Rousseff's poor track record and perceived antimarket policies made Neves a favorite of investors. Early polling showed Neves ahead of President Rousseff in mid-October. The president was increasingly seen with former president Lula in the final weeks of the campaign. In the first debate between the two candidates, Neves sharply criticized the president over the growing scandal in Petrobras; she, in turn, alleged that he would slash social programs that benefited the poor. By the third week in October, the president had outpaced Neves in the national polls. And on Sunday, October 26, by the smallest of margins, the president carried the day, winning with 51 percent of the vote against 48 percent for her opponent. The vote confirmed that Brazilian society was polarized. The poorer north and northeast had supported the president; the upper-income and more highly educated voters in the south and southeast (representing 70 percent or more of the country's GDP) had strongly endorsed her opponent.

As expected the *real* dropped to a nine-year low the day after the election and stocks plunged as investors expressed their concern over the reelection of the president. The press carefully reported that 50 percent of the value of the stock market in dollar terms had evaporated during her first term in office and the economy experienced its slowest average rate of growth since the early 1990s. It was also widely reported that Petrobras had lost 40 percent of its market value during her first administration and the scandal involving kickbacks to the PT was growing as the election results were announced.

President Rousseff begins her second administration with a precarious economy. The country, at the end of 2014, was running primary deficits with a nominal deficit approaching 4 percent of GDP. Continued low growth is expected and inflation has passed the Central Bank target of 6.5 percent by the end of the year. The question at the end of 2014 was whether or not the president and her team would read the election results as support for more of the same or view the narrow margin of victory as a wake-up call for more market-friendly, less interventionist policies in 2015.

But the last weeks of the 2014 campaign turned negative. The president's forces accused Aécio Neves, the candidate of the Social Democratic Party, of favoring a "neoliberal" or market-oriented economic program that would dilute many of the social programs instigated by the Workers Party and President Lula.

Every effort was made to portray Silva as an inexperienced candidate without the experience to govern Brazil. There is no doubt that both approaches were successful. Rousseff won the first round on October 6 with 42 percent of the vote; Neves received 34 percent; and Silva almost 20 percent. The same themes were used by the Rousseff forces in the second round of the campaign. The president refused to admit that the country faced serious economic problems. She spoke about the past and how she would replicate that record in her second term of office. The final vote was held on October 26 and Rousseff received a narrow victory with 51.6 percent of the vote; Neves took 48.4 percent. The Workers Party had prevailed—barely.

Rousseff's fall from grace

As soon as the election was over, the economic and political realities that would haunt the president as she began her second term became obvious. At the end of October 2014, interest rates were raised to 11.25 percent. Inflation had reached 6.75 percent and would continue to deteriorate during 2015; by early 2016 it had reached 10.5 percent. Unemployment began to increase at the end of 2014 and that trend would continue in the new year. The annual rate of growth of the Gross Domestic Product (GDP) fell to zero. The stock market had lost one-third of its value during her first mandate.

In hope of rescuing the economy, in January 2015, Rousseff appointed Joaquim Levy, an experienced economist, as Finance Minister. He would survive just for a year in office as he unsuccessfully tried to convince the Brazilian Congress that serious permanent fiscal adjustment was urgently required. The Workers Party in particular was rigid in its opposition to any rollback of government programs. During his time in the Finance Ministry, two of the three rating agencies downgraded Brazil's bonds to junk. This meant that many institutional investors were required to withdraw funds from Brazilian instruments. Flight capital increased as investors began to believe the fiscal crisis would deepen.

Rousseff's popularity began to drop as Brazilians began to realize that she had been less than truthful in the 2014 campaign about the state of the country's finances. Street protests occurred in March 2015 that demanded her impeachment. That theme would continue throughout 2015 and into 2016. The complicated dynamics of the Brazilian political party system guaranteed that the impeachment debate would continue into 2016. The Federal Court of Accounts, an auditing body tied to the Congress, is examining whether the president improperly used funds from giant state banks to shore up the federal budget. At the same time the National Electoral Tribunal has opened an investigation into whether or not the 2014 reelection campaign received illegal campaign donations.

The political constant in 2015–2016 was the ongoing scandal at the state-run oil company, Petrobras. Federal investigators alleged that Brazilian construction companies, a powerful lobbying group, had paid an estimated $3 billion in bribes to officials in the company for the awarding of construction contracts. To the delight of many Brazilians, the presidents of two of the largest companies were arrested in June 2015. The traditional impunity enjoyed by the political and economic elites apparently had begun to be challenged for the first time. Federal prosecutors were pursuing a number of allegations linked to the scandal. It was noted that President Rousseff had served as the chairperson of Petrobras from 2003–2010 and also served as Minister of Mines and Energy in the Lula government.

By early 2016, it became clear to many Brazilians that Rousseff's first term in office, 2009–2014, had been a disaster. Growth had disappeared. The presidential palace had pressured the central bank to reduce interest rates, fueling a credit spree among overstretched consumers who are now struggling to repay loans. Rousseff had cut taxes for certain domestic industries and imposed price controls on gasoline and electricity, creating huge losses at public energy companies. She had also expanded the lending authority of the National Development Bank (BNDES), which had already dwarfed that of the World Bank. Drawing funds from the national treasury, the bank increased taxpayer-subsidized loans to large corporations at rates that were significantly lower than those individuals could obtain from their banks.

With energy prices falling across the globe, they are soaring in Brazil as the government loosens its price controls. Residential electricity rates alone surged more than 40 percent in 2015 as the authorities tried to recoup losses at public electricity companies. It's also becoming clear that the Workers Party government overextended their dependence on the Chinese demand for Brazilian iron ore, soy, and oil. With a slowdown in the Chinese economy specifically and the world economy in general, Brazil's export markets are shrinking.

The Rousseff government has been unable to convince the Congress to legislate changes in the tax code, to cut the federal bureaucracy—which grew almost 30 percent from 2003 to 2013 to 600,000 civil servants—or to address the pension system, where laws allow many Brazilians to start receiving retirement benefits in their early 50s, even though life expectancy has increased and the fertility rate has fallen, limiting the number of young people supporting the aging population.

The government continued to lower its primary surplus targets in 2015–2016, creating uncertainty in capital markets and among foreign investors. Economist estimate that it may take years to undo the damage of the three terms in office of the Workers Party and that is without regard to whether or not President Rousseff is impeached. Her probable successor, Vice President Michel Temer, has been accused of corruption, as have the next two politicians in line to become president. The next scheduled national election is 2018.

NOTES

Chapter 1

1. H. B. Johnson, "Portuguese Settlement, 1500–1800," in *Colonial Brazil*, ed. Leslie Bethell (Cambridge, UK: Cambridge University Press, 1987), p. 27.
2. Anthony W. Marx, *Making Race and Nation: A Comparison of South Africa, the United States, and Brazil* (Cambridge, UK: Cambridge University Press, 1998), p. 27.
3. Bethell, *Colonial Brazil*, p. 67.
4. Ibid.
5. Brian P. Owensby, *Intimate Ironies: Modernity and the Making of Middle-Class Lives in Brazil* (Stanford, CA: Stanford University Press, 1999), p. 63.

Chapter 2

1. Werner Baer, *The Brazilian Economy: Growth and Development*, 7th ed. (Boulder and London: Lynne Rienner, 2014) , p. 32.
2. Ibid., p. 33.
3. Ibid., p. 37.
4. Thomas E. Skidmore, *Politics in Brazil, 1930–1964: An Experiment in Democracy* (Oxford, UK: Oxford University Press, 1970), p. 29.
5. Britta H. Crandall, *Hemispheric Giants: The Misunderstood History of U.S.–Brazilian Relations* (Lanham, MD: Rowman & Littlefield, 2011), p. 50.

Chapter 3

1. Skidmore, *Politics in Brazil*, p. xv.
2. Owensby, *Intimate Ironies*, p. 9.

3. Skidmore, *Politics in Brazil,* p. 97.
4. "The Suicide Letter of Getúlio Vargas," in *A Documentary History of Brazil,* ed. E. Bradford Burns (New York: Knopf, 1967), p. 369.

Chapter 4

1. Baer, *The Brazilian Economy,* p. 73.
2. Thomas E. Skidmore, *The Politics of Military Rule in Brazil, 1964–1985* (New York: Oxford University Press, 1988), p. 66.
3. Claudia Calirman, *Brazilian Art Under Dictatorship* (Durham, NC: Duke University Press, 2012), p. 2.

Chapter 5

1. Fernando Henrique Cardoso, *The Accidental President of Brazil: A Memoir* (New York: PublicAffairs, 2006), pp. 175–176.
2. Ibid., p. 182.
3. Ibid. p. 184.
4. Ibid., p. 185.
5. Ibid., p. 204.
6. Ibid., p. 186.
7. Albert Fishlow, *Starting Over: Brazil Since 1985* (Washington, DC: Brookings Institution Press, 2011), p. 70.
8. Fishlow, *Starting Over,* p. 47.
9. Fishlow, *Starting Over,* p. 48.

Chapter 6

1. Aline Diniz Amaral, Peter R. Kingstone, and Jonathan Krieckhaus, "The Limits of Economic Reform in Brazil," in *Democratic Brazil Revisited,* eds. Peter R. Kingstone and Timothy J. Power (Pittsburgh: University of Pittsburgh Press, 2008), p. 137.
2. Baer, *The Brazilian Economy,* p. 148.
3. Amaral et al., *Democratic Brazil Revisited,* p. 146.
4. Cardoso, *The Accidental President of Brazil,* p. 134.
5. Fishlow, *Starting Over,* pp. 126–127.
6. Baer, *The Brazilian Economy,* p. 168–169.
7. Dominic Wilson and Roopa Purushothaman, "Dreaming With BRICS: The Path to 2050," Global Economics Paper No. 99, GS Economics Workbench, October 1, 2003, Goldman Sachs, p. 1, http://www.goldmansachs.com/our-thinking/archive/archive-pdfs/brics-dream.pdf.
8. Wilson and Purushothaman, "Dreaming With BRICS", p. 10.
9. Ibid.

10. This was the general sentiment in the financial community in the years of strong economic growth in Brazil.
11. Ibid.
12. Jim O'Neill, "The Brics Economies Must Help Form World Policy," *Financial Times*, January 22, 2007.
13. David Pilling, "The Brics Bank Is a Glimpse of the Future," *Financial Times*, July 31, 2014.
14. Riordan Roett, *The New Brazil* (Washington, DC: Brookings Institution Press, 2010), p. 118.
15. Roett, *The New Brazil*, p. 118.
16. World Economic Forum, *Global Competitiveness Index, 2013–2014* (Geneva, Switzerland: World Economic Forum, 2014).
17. Getúlio Vargas Foundation, "How to Improve Education Quality," *The Brazilian Economy* 6, no. 7 (July 2014): 7.
18. Ibid.
19. Ibid.
20. Ibid.
21. Ibid., p. 11.
22. "Brazil: Education 2.0," in Getúlio Vargas Foundation, *The Brazilian Economy* 6, no. 7 (July 2014), pp. 7–14.
23. Barbara Bruns and Javier Luque, *Great Teachers: How to Raise Student Learning in Latin America and the Caribbean* (Washington, DC: World Bank, 2015), p. 47.
24. Bruns and Luque, *Great Teachers*, p. 47.

Chapter 7

1. Edmund A. Walsh School of Foreign Service, Georgetown University, *Political Database of the Americas*, Federative Republic of Brazil Electoral Results, 2010 Presidential Election, http://pdba.georgetown.edu/Elecdata/Brazil/pres10_2.html.
2. OECD, *OECD Economic Surveys: Brazil, Overview* (Paris: OECD, 2013), p. 4.
3. *OECD Economic Surveys: Brazil*, November 2015, p. 10, www.oecd.org/Brazil.
4. Juan Forero, "Brazil's Oil Euphoria Hits Reality Hard," *Washington Post*, January 6, 2014.
5. Jonathan Wheatley, "Opinion: The case for Brazil's BNDES," *Financial Times*, June 3, 2014.
6. Ibid.
7. Kenneth Rapoza, "Was Brazil's Belo Monte Dam a Bad Idea?" *Forbes*, March 7, 2014.

Chapter 8

1. Getúlio Vargas Foundation, "Can Brazil Find a Route to Competitiveness?" *The Brazilian Economy*, 6, no. 8 (August 2014): 7.
2. G. B. Martha, Jr., Elisio Contini, and Eliseu Alves, "Embrapa: Its Origins and Changes," in *The Regional Impact of National Policies: The Case of Brazil*, ed. Werner Baer (Northampton, MA: Edward Elgar, 2012), p. 204.
3. Paulo Correa and Cristiane Schmidt, "Public Research Organizations and Agricultural Development in Brazil: How Did Embrapa Get It Right?" *Economic Premise* 145 (2014), Washington, DC: World Bank Poverty Reduction and Economic Management (PREM) Network, p. 8.
4. Ibid.
5. Ibid.
6. Heinz-Peter Elstrodt, James Manyika, Jaana Remes et al., McKinsey Global Institute, "Connecting Brazil to the World: A Path to Inclusive Growth," McKinsey and Company, May 2014, pp. 47–48.
7. Getúlio Vargas Foundation, "Can Brazil Find a Route to Competitiveness?", p. 7.
8. Getúlio Vargas Foundation, Angel Gurría Interview, "Can Brazil Find a Route to Competitiveness?", pp. 20–25.
9. Heinz-Peter Elstrodt, James Manyika, Jaana Remes et al., McKinsey Global Institute, "Connecting Brazil to the World: A Path to Inclusive Growth," p. 1.
10. McKinsey Global Institute, "Connecting Brazil to the World," pp. 72–85.
11. McKinsey Global Institute, "Connecting Brazil to the World," p. 75.
12. This data is used as a general reference in discussing crime rates in Brazil.
13. This trend was confirmed in the highly contentious national election in 2014.
14. Antonio Bandeira and Josephine Bourgois, "Firearms: Protection or Risk?," Parliamentary Forum on Small Arms and Light Weapons, p. 14 http://www.parliamentaryforum.org/sites/default/files/firearms%20protection%20or%20risk.pdf.
15. Pierre-Richard Agénor and Otaviano Canuto, "Gender Equality and Economic Growth: A Framework for Policy Analysis," April 24, 2013, http://www.voxeu.org/article/gender-equality-and-economic-growth-framework-policy-analysis.

16. Fernando Henrique Cardoso, *The Accidental President of Brazil: A Memoir.* (Public Affairs, New York, 2006), pp. 213–217.
17. Ibid.

Chapter 9

1. Crandall, *Hemispheric Giants,* p. 7.
2. Roger Cohen, "An Odd Hostility in the Americas," *New York Times,* April 21, 2014.
3. Monica Hirst, *The United States and Brazil: A Long Road of Unmet Expectations* (New York and London: Routledge, 2005).
4. Roett, *The New Brazil,* p. 130.
5. CELAC, "Havana Declaration," II Cumbre, La Habana, January 28–29, 2014, p. 2. http://celac.cubaminrex.cu/sites/default/files/ficheros/havana_declaration_celac.pdf.
6. Cynthia J. Arnson and Jorge Heine, eds., *Reaching Across the Pacific: Latin America and Asia in the New Century* (Washington, DC: Woodrow Wilson Center, 2014), p. 135.

Chapter 10

1. Larry Rohter, "From Carmen Miranda to the Grateful Dead: Brazil and the United States' Musical Dialogue," *Revista,* Harvard Review of Latin America, Winter 2016, pp. 46-49.

Chapter 11

1. Simon Romero, "From Boom to Rust, Lavish Projects Are Languishing in Brazil," *New York Times,* April 12, 2014.
2. Ibid.
3. John Paul Rathbone, "Fragile Middle: Latin American Aspirations Risk Being Frustrated," *Financial Times,* April 15, 2014.
4. "Race in Brazil, Affirming a Divide," *The Economist,* January 28, 2012.
5. This trend is generally confirmed in most of the current research on race relations.
6. Estanislao Gacitúa-Marió and Michael Woolcock, eds., *Social Exclusion and Mobility in Brazil* (Washington, DC: World Bank, 2008), p. 16.
7. "Race in Brazil," *The Economist,* January 28, 2012.
8. Marlise Simons, "Brazil's Blacks Feel Bias 100 Years After Slavery," *New York Times,* May 14, 1988.

INDEX